T0313838

Conglomerate Mergers
and Market Competition

CONGLOMERATE MERGERS

and MARKET COMPETITION

BY JOHN C. NARVER

PUBLICATIONS OF
THE INSTITUTE OF BUSINESS AND ECONOMIC RESEARCH
UNIVERSITY OF CALIFORNIA

UNIVERSITY OF CALIFORNIA PRESS
Berkeley and Los Angeles 1969

University of California Press
  Berkeley and Los Angeles, California
University of California Press, Ltd.
  London, England

Copyright © 1967, by The Regents of the University of California
Second Printing, 1969
Library of Congress Catalog Card Number: 67-11444
ISBN 978-0-520-30721-6

Preface

PROFESSOR Donald F. Turner, the recently appointed U.S. Assistant Attorney General for Antitrust, published an important article on conglomerate mergers after the preparation of the present analysis. This article, "Conglomerate Mergers and Section 7 of the Clayton Act," *Harvard Law Review,* LXXVIII (May, 1965), deals with many of the same issues as this study. The present work parallels Professor Turner's in emphasizing effects on competition rather than the extra-competition issue of superconcentration in the economy. However, as to the competitive implications of conglomerate mergers, the present analysis differs substantially from Professor Turner's in terms of approach and conclusions. One difference is that the present study spells out more precisely the manner and conditions in which conglomerate mergers may weaken or strengthen competition in a market.

This writer is grateful to the Ford Foundation and the Research Program in Marketing at the Graduate School of Business Administration, University of California, Berkeley, for providing financial and administrative assistance. Particular appreciation is extended to Professors E. T. Grether and L. E. Preston for their generous accessibility as well as for their stimulation and guidance. The encouragement from my wife, Elizabeth, has been of the utmost value throughout all phases of this study.

Contents

Chapter I

INTRODUCTION

In THEIR quest for efficiency and market effectiveness, firms frequently merge. One firm's acquisition of another firm or firms has been a common phenomenon in the United States for three-quarters of a century. A concomitant of any merging—at least at the instant of merger—is an increase in the concentration of asset ownership in the economy. Mergers of competitors increase asset concentration in their market unless there is an offsetting entry of independent assets.

Ours is a society that desires economic efficiency but also cherishes decentralized economic and political processes. It has been frequently and strongly argued that increased ownership concentration, whether in specific markets or in the economy as a whole, may well run counter to a decentralized economic and political system. What are the implications of mergers for free competition in the market place? Do mergers necessarily significantly affect competition in a market? Do all three types of mergers—horizontal, vertical, and conglomerate—affect the intensity of business rivalry? Convinced that all types of mergers could affect competition, and wishing to prohibit any horizontal, vertical, or conglomerate merger which would probably and substantially lessen market competition, the Congress of the United States in 1950 passed the Celler-Kefauver Amendment to Section 7 of the Clayton Act.

Economic theory provides considerable insight into the effects of horizontal and vertical mergers on competition. But it offers much less help in the analysis of conglomerate mergers. Indeed, economists have yet to agree on a satisfactory general definition of the essential aspects of conglomerate

mergers and an adequate description of their effects on competition. For that matter, there has been relatively little
systematic research on the related questions of a theory of
diversification and a theory of mergers. The present study
attempts to determine under what conditions conglomerate
mergers—as defined below—tend to increase or decrease
competition in a market, and the factors in conglomerate
mergers tending to produce these results. The study considers the phenomena of conglomerate mergers from several
perspectives and establishes a framework for predicting their
probable competitive effects.

The key concepts briefly defined here will be more fully
developed in the chapters dealing with the phenomena to
which they refer and with the implications of their particular
formulations. For the moment, the introduction of the terms
here provides a summary preview of the subject of the study.

As used in this analysis *merger* refers to all types of acquisitions of assets or stock of part or all of another firm (or other
firms) that result in operational control of the part or the
whole of the other firm. There are legal differences between
acquisitions, mergers, and consolidations, but the distinctions
are not important for this analysis. The term "acquisition" is
sometimes used in this report as a substitute for "merger."
The important feature of merger in this discussion is transfer
of the control of business activity from one firm or firms to
another.

A *horizontal merger* is a merger of firms whose products
are viewed by buyers as virtually identical—i.e., the products
have a high cross-elasticity of demand—or of firms whose
products have a high cross-elasticity of supply. From the
standpoint of demand and supply the products in the horizontal merger are viewed as highly substitutable.

The key distinction of the *vertical merger* is a successive
functional relationship between the acquiring and acquired
firms—the product of one firm is a production input for, or

is marketed by, the other firm. In general, the merging of a supplier and a customer is a vertical merger.

A *conglomerate merger* is any merger that is neither horizontal nor vertical. The products of the acquiring and acquired firms are not competitive nor are they vertically related. Thus, a completely conglomerate merger produces a firm having a number of external markets equal to the sum of the premerger external markets of the acquiring and the acquired firms. Anything less puts the merger at least partly into a horizontal- or vertical-merger category. The number of external markets in both horizontal mergers and vertical mergers after the merger is at least one market less than before the merger.[1]

A conglomerate firm is a market-diversified firm—the firm operates in two or more separate product and/or geographic markets. Through internal expansion, the act of conglomeration or "diversification" refers to any act of increasing the number of the firm's external markets. Whereas through merger, the act of conglomeration or diversification is the gathering into one firm the independent external markets of the acquiring and acquired firms.

NODE COMMONALITY

The distinction between the three kinds of mergers—horizontal, vertical, and conglomerate—rests solely on the basis

---

[1] It is quite possible for a merger between two large, diversified firms to have horizontal, vertical, and conglomerate aspects. In such a situation, the pre-merger firms have some competing products, some vertically related products, and some which are conglomerate—neither horizontally nor vertically related. Three hypothetical mergers will help clarify the distinctions: one merger is completely horizontal, one is completely vertical, and one is completely conglomerate. For the sake of illustrative simplicity, let us assume that each of the two parties to each of the mergers is a single-product firm. Thus, each pre-merger firm sells in one external market—there are two external markets for each pair. When the pair of competing firms merge (the horizontal merger), the post-merger entity has only one external market. When the two vertically related firms merge (the vertical merger), the post-merger entity also has but one external market (it also has one internal market—selling to itself). When the two non-competing, non-vertically related firms merge (the conglomerate merger), the post-merger entity still has two external markets.

of the relationship between the products of the parties to the merger. In its strict meaning a conglomerate merger completely lacks either horizontal or vertical product relationships. Less strictly, a conglomerate merger involves *some* products having neither horizontal nor vertical relationships. Moreover, among mergers that qualify as conglomerate a considerable range of organizational relationships is to be found. The conglomerate mergers tend to fall along a spectrum in terms of commonness or similarity of component resources and activities of the two firms. This spectrum has nothing to do with sizes of the parties nor with the products themselves (the products are non-competing and non-vertically related). The spectrum is exclusively a matter of the degree of technological and resource "fit" between the merging firms.

Each firm may be viewed as a collection of component resources and activities—specific inputs, specific resources (including managerial knowledge), specific production processes, and specific distribution patterns and arrangements—in short, as a set of elements each of which has some productive output and capacity. If we designate each location of an element or any point at which several elements center as a "node," then "node" may be substituted for "element," and a firm may be conceived of as a collection of nodes—in particular, organization-activity nodes.

The concept of nodes is helpful in referring to the degree of relationship between the activities of the acquiring and acquired firms in a conglomerate merger: the degree of relationship is the degree of node commonality that exists in the particular merger, the extent to which the specific activity nodes of the two firms are jointly employable. In set-theory terms, the degree of node commonality has the same meaning as the extent of the intersection of the sets.

What are the cost implications of node commonality? As we have mentioned, each firm is a collection of component resources and activities. Frequently in a "functional" conglomerate merger (as opposed to a "pure-investment" conglomerate merger), some of the *intermediate* products and processes of the parties to the merger are identical (for reasons to be discussed later in the study). Thus, some intermediate as well as certain end products lend themselves to some degree of joint production either in fixed or variable proportions. If not as jointly produced products, one at least frequently finds products and processes of the parties incurring common costs. The extent to which these conditions are found reflects the degree of *node commonality* in the merger. In the short run, then, a degree of node commonality is a measure of the potential for performing an activity more efficiently as a merged firm than as two separate entities. When the processes are identical, costs may be lower—in effect an outward movement along a given scale curve. When the processes are not identical but may be performed jointly or with common costs, there are opportunities for efficiencies in the absorption of excess capacity. For example, the degree of node commonality in marketing suggests the amount of opportunity for lower costs in marketing activities. Specifically, a high degree of commonality in sales promotion suggests considerable potential for joint branding and joint advertising, or joint personal selling, and, probably, joint use of channels of distribution, all leading to increased efficiency in the use of promotion resources.

In the long run, node commonality implies economies of scale—a more economical organization of the total activity in the commonality. The ability to reorganize to a more economical scale differs for various activities; that is, the long run for the marketing function is probably different from the long run in the production activity. The important point about the long-run implications of node commonality is that improvement in techniques and regrouping of activities typically result in lower costs. The savings are effected exactly as in other long-run economies of scale—by reorganization to more efficient scales of activity.

The literature on conglomerate mergers sometimes refers to "degree of conglomerateness." This term designates the inverse of "degree of node commonality." Thus, a conglomerate merger in which the firms embody highly unrelated resources and activities may be said to have a "high degree of conglomerateness" or "very low node commonality." But whichever term is used, the reference is not to the products but to the organizational relationship between the merging firms.

SEQUENCE OF ANALYSIS

Chapter II presents a discussion of the magnitude of conglomeration in the American economy, the magnitude of current merger activity, and, inferentially, the magnitude of conglomeration resulting from mergers. The 1958 censuses of Business, Manufactures, and Mineral Industries and Federal Trade Commission data provide most of the information for this chapter.

Chapter III offers a legislative history of conglomerate mergers in the 1950 Celler-Kefauver Amendment to Section 7 of the Clayton Act. It attempts to discover the intent of Congress regarding conglomerate mergers, and especially to determine whether Congress had a particular kind of diversification merger in mind. The chapter also shows how the conception of conglomerate mergers changed from the time of initial interest in them to their eventual inclusion in the 1950 Act.

Chapter IV provides an analysis of the managerial decision to diversify—and specifically to diversify by merger. The discussion focuses on the general forces leading to conglomerate mergers and on the degree of node commonality typically found in diversification and, in particular, in diversification mergers. The analysis also considers the degree to which efficiencies are possible in conglomerate firms and the conditions under which the probable realization of efficiencies is greatest.

Chapter V reviews several conglomerate-merger actions instituted by the Department of Justice and the Federal Trade Commission under Section 7, with particular emphasis on the approaches used by the administrative agencies. This examination is not a legal discussion, but an analysis of the agencies' charges to deduce implications for the effects of conglomerate mergers on competition.

Chapter VI focuses on the "conglomerate market power" of a conglomerate firm, discussing what conglomerate market power is, how and when it may occur, what conditions determine its magnitude, and how it may be implemented in the market behavior of the firm.

The concluding Chapter VII deals with the critical ultimate question of this study: Under what conditions and in what direction may conglomerate mergers tend to affect competition? Two objectives are pursued in this presentation: focusing primarily on conglomerate market power, the analysis suggests the situations in which conglomerate mergers may tend to affect competition most significantly and establishes a general framework for evaluating a conglomerate merger's competitive effects.

Chapter II

RECENT TRENDS
IN CONGLOMERATION AND
CONGLOMERATE MERGER ACTIVITY

"Whereas the great merger movement of 1900 involved predominantly horizontal mergers, e.g. the sugar, powder, petroleum, tobacco, and steel trusts, many and perhaps most large mergers today are primarily among firms producing different products, operating in different geographic areas, or involve vertical relationships."[1] This statement underscores the importance of nonhorizontal mergers today and opens the door to a number of questions to be considered in this chapter. Is there increasing diversification among American industrial and business firms? Are all types of mergers on the increase? Are conglomerate mergers increasing as a percentage of total mergers? Is there any relationship between the size of the acquiring firm and number of conglomerate mergers? Many data bearing upon these questions are available and a review of the statistical aspects of merger trends affords essential background for an analysis of the impact of conglomerate mergers on competition.

MULTI-INDUSTRY ACTIVITY IN AMERICAN COMPANIES

In 1954 and 1958, single-unit, single-industry firms comprised the bulk of American business and industrial firms, and in approximately the same proportions (Table 1). In terms of employment, however, multi-unit, multi-industry firms

---

[1] Willard F. Mueller, "The Current Merger Movement and Public Policy," *The Antitrust Bulletin*, VIII, No. 4 (July–August, 1963), p. 633.

TABLE 1

NUMBER OF COMPANIES, THEIR ESTABLISHMENTS, AND THEIR EMPLOYMENT: 1958 AND 1954[a]

Type of company and item	All companies, total 1958		All companies, total 1954[b]		1954 to 1958	
	Number	Percent	Number	Percent	Absolute change	Percent change
Number of companies, total	3,151,606	100.0	2,783,977	100.0	+ 367,629	+13
Single unit	3,060,283	97.1	2,715,844	97.6	+ 344,439	+13
Multi-unit	91,323	2.9	68,133	2.4	+ 23,190	+34
Single industry	50,111	1.6	....	....	....	....
Multi-industry[c]	41,212	1.3	....	....	....	....
Number of establishments, total	3,493,770	100.0	3,074,427	100.0	+ 419,343	+14
Single unit	3,060,283	87.6	2,715,844	88.3	+ 344,439	+13
Multi-unit	433,487	12.4	358,583	11.7	+ 74,904	+21
Single industry	157,602	4.5	....	....	....	....
Multi-industry[c]	275,885	7.9	....	....	....	....
Company employment, total	30,952,000	100.0	29,497,000	100.0	+1,455,000	+ 5
Single unit	14,295,000	46.2	14,149,000	48.0	+ 146,000	+ 1
Multi-unit	16,657,000	53.8	15,348,000	52.0	+1,309,000	+ 9
Single industry	2,904,000	9.4	....	....	....	....
Multi-industry	13,753,000	44.4	....	....	....	....

[a] The data aggregate 855 (4-digit) census industry classifications involving six industry divisions: mineral, manufacturing, wholesale trade, retail trade, selected services, and public warehousing.

[b] Multi-unit companies 1954 data are not shown by single-industry and multi-industry subclassifications, as for 1958, because of significant differences in the 1954 and 1958 classification definitions.

[c] A Multi-unit company is classified as multi-industry if the establishments it owned or controlled were in more than one of the 855 (4-digit) census industry classifications.

SOURCES: Adapted from Tables A, B, and D, U.S. Bureau of the Census, *Enterprise Statistics: 1958 Part 1 General Report* (Washington, D.C.: U.S. Government Printing Office, 1963), pp. 22, 23, and 25.

are far more significant. In 1958, multi-industry firms comprised only 1.3 percent of the total of more than 3.1 million companies but accounted for 44.4 percent of the total company employment.

A tentative suggestion can be developed about the nature of changes in multi-unit, multi-industry companies from 1954 to 1958. According to Gort (at the 4-digit classification level covering the same six industry divisions as in Table 1) multi-industry companies in 1954 comprised only .246 percent of all companies,[2] whereas Table 1, as mentioned, shows that in 1958 multi-industry companies accounted for 1.3 percent of all companies. Several other comparisons between 1954 and 1958 data are of interest. Gort says that in 1954 multi-industry companies comprised approximately 10 percent of all multi-unit companies;[3] a calculation from Table 1 shows that in 1958 multi-industry companies accounted for approximately 45 percent of all multi-unit companies. Table 1 also shows that multi-industry employment in 1958 comprised 44.4 percent of all company employment, whereas Gort's data indicate that in 1954 multi-industry employment was only 38.37 percent of the total for all companies.[4] Moreover, in 1954 multi-industry employment comprised 73.74 percent of multi-unit employment,[5] whereas a calculation from Table 1 indicates approximately 83 percent in 1958. These comparisons suggest the substantial and increasing importance in the aggregate of multi-industry companies as defined at the 4-digit census classification level.

It is of further interest to study the aggregate data of Table 1 broken down into the six industry divisions in Table 2. The importance of the multi-industry company is particularly evident in the manufacturing sector. In 1958 multi-industry firms in manufacturing accounted for only 2.6 percent of all

---

[2] Michael Gort, *Diversification and Integration in American Industry* (Princeton: Princeton University Press for the National Bureau of Economic Research, 1962), Table 6, p. 29.
[3] *Ibid.*
[4] *Ibid.*
[5] *Ibid.*

manufacturing firms but provided 59 percent of all manufacturing employment. The average numbers of employees
and establishments for multi-industry manufacturing firms
in 1958 were 1,440 and 14.9 respectively.[6] An interesting contrast to manufacturing is provided by the retail trade sector.
As Table 2 indicates, the total number of retail firms in 1958
was approximately 1.69 million, about six times the number
of manufacturing firms; but the number of multi-industry
retail firms was approximately 2.8 times the number of multi-
industry manufacturing firms. With far fewer firms, multi-
industry manufacturing firms' employment was more than
four times as great as that in multi-industry retail firms. As
contrasted to the previous statistic for multi-industry manufacturing firms, the average numbers of employees and establishments for multi-industry retail firms in 1958 were 120
and 5.5 respectively.[7]

Tables 1 and 2, and later tables, afford a degree of comparison between 1954 and 1958. But caution should be exercised
in considering these comparisons lest too much be read into
the data. For instance:

> Comparisons are also affected by companies which signifi-
> cantly changed their industry "mix" between 1954 and 1958
> (through internal growth, merger, acquisition, etc.), with
> resulting shifts in their industry category classifications. Such
> classification "transfers" of companies from category "A" to
> category "B," for example, constitute part of the observed net
> 1954–1958 changes in the data totals of both categories . . .
> Although 1954 and 1958 were both years in which business
> recessions ended, the April 1958 "turning point" occurred at
> higher levels of gross national product, nonfarm employment,
> industrial production, retail sales, etc., than the comparable
> turning point in August 1954. Furthermore, the eight months
> of business recovery in 1958 showed a much stronger rebound
> than the four months of recovery in 1954.[8]

---

[6] *Enterprise Statistics: 1958 Part 1 General Report* (Washington, D. C.:
U.S. Government Printing Office, 1963), Table C, p. 24.
[7] *Ibid.*
[8] *Ibid.*, p. 23.

TABLE 2

NUMBER AND PERCENT DISTRIBUTION OF COMPANIES,
THEIR ESTABLISHMENTS, AND THEIR EMPLOYMENT, BY INDUSTRY DIVISION
AND BY TYPE OF COMPANY: 1958 AND 1954[a]

Item	Mineral industries			
	1958		1954[b]	
	Number	Percent	Number	Percent
Number of companies, total	30,133	100.0	30,274	100.0
Single unit	28,267	93.8	28,256	93.3
Multi-unit	1,866	6.2	2,018	6.7
Single industry	1,033	3.4	....	....
Multi-industry[c]	833	2.8	....	....
Number of establishments, total	36,613	100.0	37,181	100.0
Single unit	28,267	77.2	28,256	76.0
Multi-unit	8,346	22.8	8,925	24.0
Single industry	2,794	7.6	....	....
Multi-industry[c]	5,552	15.2	....	....
Company employment, total[d]	575,000	100.0	597,000	100.0
Single unit	249,000	43.3	255,000	42.7
Multi-unit	326,000	56.7	341,000	57.1
Single industry	56,000	9.8	....	....
Multi-industry[c]	270,000	46.9	....	....
	Retail trade			
	1958		1954[b]	
	Number	Percent	Number	Percent
Number of companies, total	1,688,322	100.0	1,542,982	100.0
Single unit	1,641,091	97.2	1,503,954	97.5
Multi-unit	47,231	2.8	39,028	2.5
Single industry	27,388	1.6	....	....
Multi-industry[c]	19,843	1.2	....	....
Number of establishments, total	1,839,234	100.0	1,677,000	100.0
Single unit	1,641,091	89.2	1,503,954	89.7
Multi-unit	198,143	10.8	173,046	10.3
Single industry	88,599	4.8	....	....
Multi-industry[c]	109,544	6.0	....	....
Company employment, total[d]	8,034,000	100.0	7,217,000	100.0
Single unit	4,802,000	59.8	4,425,000	61.3
Multi-unit	3,232,000	40.2	2,791,000	38.7
Single industry	861,000	10.7	....	....
Multi-industry[c]	2,372,000	29.5	....	....

[a] Detail may not add to totals because of rounding.

[b] Multi-unit companies 1954 data are not shown by single-industry and multi-industry subclassifications because of significant differences in the 1954 and 1958 definitions of these classifications.

[c] A multi-unit company is classified as multi-industry if the establishments it owned or controlled were in more than one of the (4-digit) 855 different Census industry classifications.

TABLE 2 (continued)

Companies classified in:							
Manufacturing				Wholesale trade			
1958		1954[b]		1958		1954[b]	
Number	Percent	Number	Percent	Number	Percent	Number	Percent
269,834	100.0	263,103	100.0	213,054	100.0	185,067	100.0
258,210	95.7	255,035	96.9	198,711	93.3	176,485	95.4
11,624	4.3	8,068	3.1	14,343	6.7	8,582	4.6
4,488	1.7	....	....	7,385	3.5	....	....
7,136	2.6	....	....	6,958	3.3	....	....
379,896	100.0	356,741	100.0	246,195	100.0	211,092	100.0
258,210	68.0	255,035	71.5	198,711	93.3	176,485	83.6
121,686	32.0	101,706	28.5	47,464	6.7	34,607	16.4
15,008	4.0	....	....	21,107	3.5	....	....
106,678	28.1	....	....	26,357	3.3	....	....
17,273,000	100.0	17,251,000	100.0	2,101,000	100.0	1,989,000	100.0
5,625,000	32.6	6,140,000	35.6	1,474,000	70.2	1,457,000	73.3
11,648,000	67.4	11,111,000	64.4	626,000	29.8	532,000	26.7
1,371,000	7.9	....	....	275,000	13.1	....	....
10,278,000	59.4	....	....	352,000	16.7	....	....
Selected services				Public warehousing			
1958		1954[b]		1958		1954[b]	
Number	Percent	Number	Percent	Number	Percent	Number	Percent
942,804	100.0	755,859	100.0	7,459	100.0	6,692	100.0
926,990	98.3	745,668	98.7	7,014	94.0	6,446	96.3
15,814	1.7	10,191	1.3	445	6.0	246	3.7
9,599	1.0	....	....	218	2.9	....	....
6,215	0.7	....	....	227	3.0	....	....
983,295	100.0	784,972	100.0	8,557	100.0	7,441	100.0
926,990	94.3	745,668	95.0	7,014	82.0	6,446	86.6
56,305	5.7	39,304	5.0	1,543	18.0	995	13.4
29,465	3.0	....	....	629	7.4	....	....
26,840	2.7	....	....	914	10.7	....	....
2,869,000	100.0	2,352,000	100.0	100,000	100.0	91,000	100.0
2,080,000	72.5	1,803,000	76.7	65,000	65.4	68,000	74.7
789,000	27.5	550,000	23.4	35,000	34.6	22,000	24.2
330,000	11.5	....	....	11,000	11.3	....	....
459,000	16.0	....	....	23,000	23.3	....	....

[d] Company employment figures rounded.

SOURCE: Adapted from Tables A and B, U.S. Bureau of the Census, *Enterprise Statistics: 1958 Part 1 General Report* (Washington, D.C.: U.S. Government Printing Office, 1963), pp. 22 and 23.

It is, then, advisable to deal only with substantial changes in totals and to consider conclusions about them as of only tentative significance. In many instances, the absolute change is of less interest than the direction of change.

With these cautions in mind, we may further consider 1954–1958 changes in the numbers of companies and establishments, and in employment (Table 3). Comparable data on 1954 and 1958 totals of multi-unit, single-industry firms and multi-unit, multi-industry firms are particularly interesting because in many instances they are probably conservative indicators. That is, the scheme does not classify a multi-unit firm as being multi-industry unless the secondary activity or activities involve at least ten employees. Thus, small secondary activities in large firms or relatively large secondary activities in small firms are ignored. By the same token, activities other than those of the six divisions featured in the census are not included; hence the percentage changes may have a downward bias if such activities have increased since 1954, and *vice versa* if they have decreased.

Possible bias notwithstanding, Table 3 suggests an approximately 59 percent increase in all multi-industry firms while all firms (and all single-unit firms) were increasing only about 13 percent. In manufacturing, multi-industry firms increased 40 percent but the over-all increase in the number of firms was only 3 percent. Wholesale trade, retail trade, and selected services all had gains greater than the all-industries gain in multi-industry firms, especially the latter two sectors. Multi-industry enterprises in retail trade and selected services increased 93 percent while all enterprises in each classification were gaining only 9 percent and 25 percent respectively.

Multi-industry companies in each division showed employment gains—up to 63 percent in selected services. At the same time, company employment in all industries increased only 5 percent. The only gains in the mineral industries sector were registered by multi-industry firms. In each category (number of companies, establishments, and employment), the total multi-industry gains were at least twice as large as

TABLE 3

1954 to 1958 Percent Change in Number of Companies, Establishments, and Employment, by Type of Company and Industry Division

Number of companies, establishments, and employment by type of company	All industries total	Mineral industries	Manufacturing	Wholesale trade[a]	Retail trade	Selected services
1954-1958 percent change in:						
Number of companies, total	+13	−1	+3	+15	+9	+25
Single unit	+13	0	+1	+12	+9	+24
Multi-unit	+34	−8	+44	+68	+21	+55
Single industry[b]	+31	−13	+47	+67	+18	+53
Multi-industry[b]	+59	+15	+40	+69	+93	+93
Number of establishments, total	+14	−2	+6	+17	+10	+25
Single unit	+13	0	+1	+12	+9	+24
Multi-unit	+21	−7	+20	+38	+15	+43
Single industry[b]	+14	−29	+15	+46	+4	+36
Multi-industry[b]	+31	+33	+21	+17	+46	+79
Company employment, total	+5	−4	0	+9	+11	+22
Single unit	+1	−3	−9	+4	+9	+15
Multi-unit	+9	−5	+5	+24	+16	+44
Single industry[b]	−8	−41	−14	+24	−13	+30
Multi-industry[b]	+14	+18	+9	+23	+40	+63

a Public warehousing figures are included in wholesale trade because of the relatively small number of companies, establishments, and employees in the former.

b For purposes of comparability with 1954 figures, 1958 totals of single-industry and multi-industry multi-unit companies were retabulated for this table to conform to the 1954-type-of-industry classification system. In 1954, a multi-unit company reporting employment in other than its primary industry was nevertheless regarded as a single-industry multi-unit company if each of its secondary industries involved fewer than 10 employees or was an out-of-census-scope activity.

SOURCE: Table D, U.S. Bureau of the Census, *Enterprise Statistics: 1958 Part 1 General Report* (Washington, D.C.: U.S. Government Printing Office, 1963), p. 25.

total all-industries gains. The conclusion that multi-industry operations are of increasing importance in the American economy appears inescapable.

DIVERSIFICATION PATTERNS

"Diversification" in the census tabulations represents the extent to which economic enterprise includes activities outside a primary industry classification. Diversification data presented in Table 4 are based on only 122 industry categories —an overinclusive classification system. However, the use of the broad system was necessary in this instance to permit inter-year comparisons. To the extent diversification patterns show up in such broad categories, they indicate substantial departures from primary product bases.

The industry specialization ratios in Table 4 suggest the extent to which companies classified in a particular industry limit their activity to that primary industry. The inverse of the specialization ratio represents the extent of diversification. In 1954, the specialization ratio for all industries in the 122 categories was 89.5 percent; in 1958 the all-industries ratio was 88.3 percent. The over-all industry specialization ratio in 1958 was 98.7 percent of its 1954 level. Public warehousing shows the greatest increase of diversification, with a 1958 specialization ratio only 94.6 percent of the 1954 level. This division also shows increased employment in secondary-industry categories to a level 579 percent of its 1954 level, whereas the over-all increase in secondary-industry employment was 116 percent. The total growth pattern of multi-industry companies may be seen as greater employment gains in their secondary-industry categories relative to lesser *gains* in the primary-industry category. In fact it was only in the mineral industries and manufacturing divisions that employment in primary-industry categories actually decreased over the four-year period.[9]

---

[9] Gort computed the average primary industry specialization for 111 large firms based on the ratio of primary 4-digit industry payrolls to total manufacturing payrolls for 1947 and 1954. While the basis of his ratios is different

TABLE 4

1954–1958 Indexes of Change in Company Employment and Industry Specialization Ratios by 1954 Industry Categories

Item	Companies classified in:						
	All industries total	Mineral industries	Manufacturing	Wholesale trade	Retail trade	Selected services	Public Warehousing
Company employment							
1958 "Industry Specialization Ratio"[a]	88.3	89.9	81.4	95.7	96.4	98.2	93.5
1954 "Industry Specialization Ratio"[a]	89.5	93.9	83.8	96.3	96.8	99.0	98.8
1954–1958 Indexes of change (1954 = 100.0)							
In company employment, total	104.9	96.3	99.8	108.9	111.3	122.0	110.3
In "primary" industry categories of companies[b]	103.0	91.4	95.7	108.4	110.7	120.9	104.3
In "secondary" industry categories	116.1	159.0	113.3	127.0	124.8	223.3	579.1
In central administrative offices, sales branches, etc.[c]	117.5	119.0	118.0	91.1	116.6	127.1	128.7
In "Industry Specialization Ratio"	98.7	95.7	97.1	99.4	99.6	99.2	94.6

[a] Defined as: primary employment of companies in the industry category (i.e., employment in establishments classified in the same industry category as the owning company)/total employment of companies in the industry category, excluding employment in central administrative offices, auxiliaries, and manufacturers' sales branches and sales offices.

[b] The primary industry category is that industry in which the company is predominantly represented (in terms of payroll or value added) among all its industry categories in which it has one or more establishments.

[c] Included are central administrative offices, auxiliaries, and manufacturers' sales branches and sales offices.

Sources: Adapted from Table G, U.S. Bureau of the Census, *Enterprise Statistics: 1958 Part 1 General Report* (Washington, D.C.: U.S. Government Printing Office, 1963), p. 28.

In manufacturing, the 1954 industry specialization ratio of 83.8 (or a diversification ratio of 16.2) is the lowest of all categories, substantially lower than that year's 98.8 ratio for public warehousing, the highest specialization ratio. Given its highly specialized base in 1954, it is thus easy to see how the latter sector could account for such a high index of *change* in secondary activities.

Table 5 gives a breakdown of diversification into 855 (4-digit) census industries for 1958. At this level of classification, industry specialization ratios fell below 75 percent for 109 (one-fourth) of the 428 manufacturing industries, with 27 industries having specialization ratios of less than 50 percent. Perhaps of even greater significance than the ratios is the fact that the companies classified in the 109 low-specialization manufacturing industries accounted for more than 7 million (41 percent) of the 17.3 million employees reported by all manufacturing firms. And the companies in the 27 manufacturing industries with the lowest specialization ratios accounted for more than 2 million employees.

Nine of the 65 mineral industries in the 1958 census had specialization ratios of less than 75 percent. In these industries, however, the low-specialization companies accounted for only one-eighth of the total mineral-extracting employment.

In contrast to manufacturing and the mineral industries, most of the individual wholesale and retail trades and selected services indicated high specialization ratios. Of the 347

---

from that in Table 4 and elsewhere in this analysis, the percent change in the average specialization ratio for all companies from 1947 to 1954 is of interest. Computing from his data, the 1954 all-company ratio for 111 large enterprises is 92.7 percent of its 1947 level, a more marked change than the 98.7 1954–1958 index of change shown in Table 4. The greater magnitude of the former is explicable on at least two counts: (1) Gort's data are based on a small (111 firm) sample of large enterprises, and, as Gort points out, size of firm seemingly is positively related to the number of industries in which companies maintained activities; and (2) large firms, in some cases rather specialized for the defense effort, came out of World War II with capital to invest in market expansion and diversification. See Gort, *op. cit.*, p. 7, Table 23, p. 61, and pp. 65 ff.

TABLE 5
1958 Diversification Patterns, (4-Digit) Industries

1958 Census industry division and item	1958 Census industries total	Census industries (4-digit), by 1958 "Industry Specialization Ratio"			
		95 percent and over	75 to 94 percent	50 to 74 percent	Under 50 percent
Number of Census industries, total	855	439	291	97	28
Mineral industries	65	29	27	8	1
Manufacturing	428	130	189	82	27
Public warehousing	15	11	4	...	...
Wholesale trade	129	95	32	2	...
Retail trade	126	93	29	4	...
Selected services	92	81	10	1	...
Company Employment in Census industries (in percent)	100	42	35	16	7
Mineral industries	100	9	78	12	a
Manufacturing	100	17	42	29	12
Public warehousing	100	60	40	...	...
Wholesale trade	100	70	29	1	...
Retail trade	100	75	24	1	...
Selected services	100	85	15	a	...

a Less than 0.5 percent.
Source: U.S. Bureau of the Census, *Enterprise Statistics: 1958 Part 1 General Report* (Washington, D.C.: U.S. Government Printing Office), 1963, p. 29.

kinds of businesses in the three sectors, only 7 showed specialization ratios of less than 75 percent in 1958, with employment amounting to less than one-half percent of the combined 13 million total employment in the three sectors.[10]

The extent and significance of diversification become clearer as one investigates less-inclusive industry classifications. The Federal Trade Commission has made a preliminary tabulation of the number of 2-digit, 3-digit, 4-digit, and 5-digit classifications in which each of the 1,000 largest manufacturing corporations appeared. The tabulation indicated a high degree of diversification at the narrow 5-digit product level, but a substantially smaller degree at the broader 2-digit industry group level. Examples of 5-digit product classifications are softwood plywood, margarine, roasted coffee, and

---

[10] *Enterprise Statistics*, pp. 29–30.

lace goods. Examples of 2-digit industry groups are food and kindred products, chemicals, and transportation equipment.

According to the FTC tabulations, fewer than 5 percent of the 1,000 largest manufacturing companies were engaged in the production of goods confined to a single 5-digit product class, but more than 25 percent manufacture products included entirely in a single 2-digit industry group. Only 21 percent of these 1,000 companies were engaged in the production of as few as four 5-digit products, but 73 percent accounted for their total output in four or fewer 2-digit industry groups. While these data do not provide a precise picture of the structure of narrowly defined industries, they do show manufacturing concentration in a number of more-or-less closely related industries.[11] (The rationale for the devel-

TABLE 6

Primary 4-Digit Industry Employment to Total Company
Employment for Multi-Industry Companies in Manufacturing

1958 Specialization ratio of multi-industry companies[a]	Census industries (4-digit) in manufacturing			
	Number	Percent	Cumulative	
			Number	Percent
All manufacturing industries, total	428	100.0	—	—
Industries with no multi-industry companies	14	3.3	14	3.3
Industries with multi-industry company specialization ratio of				
90 percent or more	28	6.5	42	9.8
75 to 89 percent	111	26.0	153	35.8
50 to 74 percent	191	44.7	344	80.5
25 to 49 percent	71	16.5	415	97.0
Less than 25 percent	13	3.0	428	100.0

[a] The "multi-industry company specialization ratio" is defined as: primary company employment (employment in establishments classified in the same industry as the company) / total multi-industry company employment (*excluding* employment in sales branches, sales offices, central administrative offices and auxiliaries).

Source: Adapted from U.S. Bureau of the Census, *Enterprise Statistics: 1958 Part 1 General Report* (Washington, D.C.: U.S. Government Printing Office, 1963), p. 4.

---

[11] Willard F. Mueller makes this point. See "Concentration and Mergers in American Manufacturing," Statement before the Subcommittee on Antitrust and Monopoly of the Committee on the Judiciary, U.S. Senate, July 2, 1964, p. 16.

opment of this pattern will be discussed in Chapter V.)

Table 6 provides an interesting supplement to these data, showing at the 4-digit level the extent to which the activities of multi-industry firms in manufacturing (not to be confused with "industry specialization" in Table 5) were concentrated in their primary industry in 1958. Roughly one-third (153) of the 428 4-digit industries in manufacturing encompassed at least 75 percent of the establishment employment of their multi-industry companies. Approximately one-fifth (84) of the industries had multi-industry specialization ratios of less than 50 percent, and only 3 percent (13 industries) had multi-industry companies so broadly diversified that their "primary" industry classification failed to account for even 25 percent of their employment. In three of the 13 industries with the lowest multi-industry company specialization, total employment in the industry exceeded 100,000. These three were inorganic chemicals, "not elsewhere classified" (2819); transformers (3612); and household refrigerators (3632).[12]

Industry specialization ratios are based on single-industry firms as well as multi-industry firms. As a comparison of Tables 5 and 6 indicates, these ratios tend to he higher than multi-industry company specialization ratios. Only approximately 25 percent of all manufacturing industries had specialization ratios of less than 75 percent whereas approximately 64 percent of all manufacturing industries had multi-industry company specialization ratios of less than 75 percent.

TRENDS IN MERGER ACTIVITY

Over-all merger activity

Since the present research on mergers draws from different compilations of merger activity discrepancies in the totals for identical periods were encountered. There is, however, general consistency regarding relative changes in merger activity and trends, and the discrepancies raise no serious difficulties

---

[12] *Enterprise Statistics*, p. 4.

for the present discussion since we are not concerned with absolute magnitudes.

The Federal Trade Commission, in a 1955 report, noted that although its "figures are probably correct as to trend," the underlying source materials used do not include all mergers and acquisitions. The Commission went on to report that since 1949 the pace of important mergers and acquisitions had been rising, with the number reported in financial manuals in 1954 reaching 3 times the number reported in 1949. The 1954 total was just slightly smaller than the number reported for either 1946 or 1947, when merger activity reached a postwar peak.[13]

Table 7 presents the merger data for manufacturing and

TABLE 7

MERGERS AND ACQUISITIONS IN MANUFACTURING AND MINING
BY YEARS, 1919–1962

Year	Annual total	Year	Annual total	Year	Annual total
1919	438	1934	101	1949	126
1920	760	1935	130	1950	219
1921	487	1936	126	1951	235
1922	309	1937	124	1952	288
1923	311	1938	110	1953	295
1924	368	1939	87	1954	387
1925	554	1940	140	1955	525
1926	856	1941	111	1956	537
1927	870	1942	118	1957	490
1928	1,058	1943	213	1958	457
1929	1,245	1944	324	1959	656
1930	799	1945	333	1960	635
1931	464	1946	419	1961	671
1932	203	1947	404	1962	672
1933	120	1948	223		

SOURCES: 1919–1961: *Mergers and Superconcentration*, Staff Report of the Select Committee on Small Business, U.S. Congress, House, 87th Cong., November 8, 1962, p. 266; 1962: Charles F. Phillips, Jr., and George R. Hall, "Economic and Legal Aspects of Merger Litigation, 1951–1962," *University of Houston Business Review*, X (Fall 1963), p. 2.

[13] Federal Trade Commission, *Report on Corporate Mergers and Acquisitions* (Washington: U.S. Government Printing Office, May 1955), pp. 2–3.

mining reported by the Commission in 1955 and subsequently. Merger activity in these two sectors has been high since the mid-forties, and particularly since the mid-fifties. A separate FTC tabulation for manufacturing and mining and other acquisitions for the years 1959–1963 is presented in Table 8. The latter data are presented separately because of their discrepancy of detail.

Table 8 underscores the predominant role of manufacturing and mining in the scheme of over-all merger totals—with manufacturing bearing the major influence, as Table 9 indicates for the years 1946–1954. While the totals for manufacturing and mining mergers shown in Table 9 differ from the corresponding manufacturing and mining totals in Table 7, the directions of change evident in the two tables are the same. The primary reason for the data differences lies in differences of definitions of "control" and "acquisition."

With Tables 8 and 9 strongly suggesting the dominant role of manufacturing in the overall picture of business and industrial merger activity, Table 10 gives a breakdown of the over-all manufacturing and mining acquisitions for 1951–1961 in terms of acquisitions by the 500 largest manufacturing and mining firms. The 3,404 mergers detailed in Table 10 constitute approximately two-thirds of the total of 5,176 mergers

TABLE 8

TOTAL ACQUISITIONS BY CERTAIN CLASSIFICATIONS
AND BY YEARS, 1959–1963[a]

	Year				
Item	1963	1962	1961	1960	1959
Total acquisitions	1311	1260	1234	1012	1050
Manufacturing and mining	1018	724	759	700	719
Total nonmanufacturing	180	371	342	189	186
Wholesale and retail	123	272	248	144	147
Service and other	57	99	94	45	39
Partial acquisitions	113	165	133	123	145

[a] The Commission emphasizes that the tabulated acquisitions should not be considered as firm figures either on completed mergers or acquisitions consummated.

SOURCE: Federal Trade Commission, *News Summary* (April 29, 1964).

TABLE 9

NUMBER AND PERCENT OF ACQUISITIONS BY SECTOR OF ACQUIRING FIRM
AND BY YEARS, 1946–1954

	Sector						
	Manufacturing		Mining		Other[a]		Annual
Year	Number	Percent	Number	Percent	Number	Percent	total
1946	360	85.7	8	1.9	52	12.4	420
1947	256	80.0	15	4.7	49	15.3	320
1948	251	85.1	14	1.4	30	13.6	295
1949	180	89.6	2	1.0	19	9.5	201
1950	252	87.8	6	2.1	29	10.1	287
1951	286	88.1	10	3.1	29	8.9	325
1952	313	82.7	8	2.1	57	15.2	378
1953	329	75.5	7	1.6	100	22.9	436
1954	453	87.1	13	2.5	54	10.4	520
Totals	2,680		83		419		3,182
average percentages		84.2		2.6		13.2	

[a] "Other" includes distributive and service trades. The high magnitude of acquisitions in 1953 is due to 56 acquisitions by one jewelry firm.

SOURCE: John S. Dydo, "Inter-Industry Mergers, 1946–1954," unpublished doctoral dissertation, University of California (Berkeley), 1962, Table II-7, p. 51.

reported in Table 7 for 1951–1961. Moreover, the largest 250 firms accounted for 2,263 mergers—approximately 44 percent of the total for the eleven years.

The finding of 66 percent contribution to total mining and manufacturing mergers by the 500 largest industrial firms—smallest asset size in excess of $15 million[14]—is consistent with a FTC finding given in the 1955 report: nearly two-thirds of the reported acquisitions during 1948–1954 were made by companies with assets of $10 million or more.[15] A calculation based on the data in Table 9 shows that 65 percent (2,063 out of 3,182) of the total mergers for 1946–1954 were instances in which the acquiring firms had assets of $10 million or more.[16] Thus, the three studies are essentially consistent.

---

[14] *Mergers and Superconcentration*, Staff Report of the Select Committee on Small Business, U.S. Congress, House, 87th Cong., November 8, 1962, Table 7, p. 23.

[15] FTC, *Report on Corporate Mergers and Acquisitions*, pp. 2–3.

[16] There is probably, as noted earlier, some upward bias in any percent-of-

TABLE 10
MERGER ACTIVITY OF 500 LARGEST INDUSTRIALS, 1951–1961, BY DIMINISHING SIZE GROUPS

Sales size (rank)	50's	100's	200's	250's
			Distribution by:	
Largest 50	471			
51–100	413	Largest 100 884		
101–150	746			
151–200	313	Next 100 1,059	Largest 200 1,943	
201–250	320			Largest 250 2,263
251–300	257	Next 100 577		
301–350	250			
351–400	203	Next 100 453	Next 200 1,030	
401–450	237			
Smallest 50	194	Next 100 431		Next 250 1,141
TOTAL of 500				3,404

SOURCE: *Mergers and Superconcentration*, Staff Report of the Select Committee on Small Business, U.S. Congress, House, 87th Cong, November 8, 1962, Table 7, p. 23.

On the average the 500 largest industrials acquired 6.8 companies per firm during the eleven-year period. Sixty firms made no acquisitions; 227 companies made from 1 to 5 acquisitions; 137 made from 6 to 10 acquisitions; 54 firms made from 11 to 20 acquisitions; 16 firms made from 21 to 50 acquisitions; 4 firms made from 51 to 100 acquisitions; and 2 made more than 100 acquisitions each.[17]

Conglomerate merger activity

Some available data suggest the approximate proportion of total merger activity comprised by conglomerate mergers. To be sure, mergers are not easily broken down into categories, for mergers between integrated multi-product companies tend frequently to fall into all three classes—horizontal, vertical, and conglomerate. It is possible, however, to make rough estimates.

In its 1947 report, the FTC characterized 22 percent of the mergers from January 1940 to December 1946 as conglomerate mergers.[18] And in a 1948 report, the Commission designated as conglomerate slightly more than 21 percent of the 2,062 manufacturing and mining mergers reported for 1940–1947; horizontal mergers comprised approximately 62 percent and vertical mergers about 17 percent.[19]

Table 11 shows a merger breakdown by type and by asset size of the acquiring firms for 1946 to 1954. Horizontal mergers dominate all size classes, constituting at least 50 percent

---

total-activity computation based on the data in Table 10. The FTC admits that the totals are probably not wholly inclusive of all merger activity in the years reported. Understatement of the total deflates the denominator, thereby imputing too high a relative activity to large firms. However, the omissions may not be important, for the Commission totals are based on reports recorded in the financial manuals (such as *Standard and Poor's Corporations* and *Moody's Industrials*) supplemented by listings of acquisitions in Federal Trade Commission and Antitrust Division complaints.

[17] *Mergers and Superconcentration*, p. 23.

[18] U.S., Congress, *The Present Trend of Corporate Mergers and Acquisitions*, Document 17, 80th Cong., 1st Sess., 1947, p. 12.

[19] U.S., Federal Trade Commission, *The Merger Movement, A Summary Report*, (Washington: U.S. Government Printing Office, 1948), pp. 30–31.

of all mergers in each year. However, their relative importance declines from 66.8 percent in 1947 to 51.4 percent in
1954. Conglomerate mergers (listed as diversification) on the
other hand increased numerically every year and increased
proportionately from 11.3 percent in 1947 to 30 percent in
1954.[20] For the entire period, conglomerate mergers in this
study constituted approximately 21 percent of the total mergers, almost the same proportion the FTC found for 1940 to
1947. But since 1954 led the 9-year period with 520 mergers
(Table 9), the conglomerate merger proportion of 30 percent
for that year is clearly a significant numerical and relative increase over the preceding years. All in all, the evidence
indicates a definite shift in the merger pattern from the heavy
preponderance of horizontal and vertical mergers in the mid-

TABLE 11

1946–1954 MERGERS BY ASSET SIZE OF ACQUIRING FIRMS
AND BY KIND OF MERGER

Asset Size (millions of dollars)	Kind of Merger				
	H	V	D	R	Totals
1–4.9	379	79	122	29	609
5–9.9	307	83	98	22	510
10–24.9	438	104	153	22	717
25–49.9	276	84	88	9	457
50 and over	475	194	204	16	889
TOTALS	1,875	544	665	98	3,182

H= Horizontal Merger—merger of identical products or "reasonably close
demand substitutes."
V= Vertical Merger—merger in which the product of one of the parties
was used in substantial amounts by the other.
D= Diversification Merger—merger resulting in production or sale of a good
or service new to one of the parties and not involving a vertical relationship.
R= Residual—merger not classified because of insufficient information to
determine type.
SOURCE: John S. Dydo, "Inter-Industry Mergers, 1946–1964," Unpublished
doctoral dissertation, University of California (Berkeley), 1962, Table II-5,
p. 46.

---

[20] John S. Dydo, "Inter-Industry Mergers, 1946–1954," unpublished doctoral dissertation, University of California (Berkeley), 1962, Table II-7, p. 47.

forties to an increasingly significant emphasis on conglomerate mergers in the early fifties.

The importance of this shift is given further emphasis in
an analysis, in the FTC's 1955 report, of 1,773 manufacturing
and mining mergers consummated during 1948–1954. The
Commission noted seven general kinds of advantages conferred on the acquiring company: (1) additional capacity
to supply a market already supplied by the acquirer (observed in 2 acquisitions out of 5); (2) lengthened product
lines (1 out of 4); (3) product diversification (1 out of 4);
(4) facilities to produce goods formerly purchased (1 out
of 8); (5) facilities to process or distribute goods formerly
sold (1 out of 10); (6) facilities in markets not previously
served, but of the same type already owned (1 out of 10);
(7) other advantages (empty plants, patents, or a valuable
corporate shell, etc.) (1 out of 10).[21]

Of these seven advantages, three clearly relate to conglomerate mergers—lengthened product lines, product diversification, and market extensions. (Chapters III and V elabo-
rate this theme.) Many mergers the Commission analyzed
conferred multiple advantages on the acquiring company,
and the Commission does not indicate how many mergers
possessed solely conglomerate, horizontal, or vertical elements. If we assume that the advantages of lengthened product lines, product diversification, and market extension occurred only in the same mergers, then at least 25 percent of
the mergers were in part or whole conglomerate (other advantages may have been present as well). However, the
market-extension advantage probably did not always appear
concurrently with either of the other two advantages; and it
is almost as probable that lengthened product lines and product diversification did not always occur simultaneously.
Thus it is safe to conclude that mergers having some conglomerate elements probably comprised even more than 25

<hr>

[21] FTC, *Report on Corporate Mergers and Acquisitions*, p. 7.

percent of the manufacturing and mining mergers consummated from 1948 to 1954. On the other hand, because of the "overlap" of lengthened product lines and product diversification, it is difficult to conceive of a ratio much higher than 40 to 50 percent for this period.

Finally, it is of interest to determine whether there is any relationship between size of acquiring firm and the incidence of conglomerate mergers. Using the data of the study reviewed earlier (3,182 mergers from 1946 to 1954), Table 12 shows classes of conglomerate mergers as percentages of all mergers and as percentages of total conglomerate mergers, by asset size of the acquiring firm. Although the size groupings in the table are not equally representative of total merger activity, several observations may be made.

We can calculate from Table 12 that conglomerate mergers by firms with assets of $10 million or more comprised 21.57 percent of the total, as contrasted to a 20.54 percent conglomerate merger average for all firms. Also, whereas 64.8 percent of all mergers were accounted for by acquiring firms

TABLE 12

CONGLOMERATE MERGERS BY ASSET SIZE OF ACQUIRING FIRM
AS PERCENT OF TOTAL MERGERS AND AS PERCENT OF
ALL CONGLOMERATE MERGERS[a]

Asset Size of Acquiring Firm (millions of dollars)	Total Mergers			Conglomerate Mergers	
	(a)	(b)	(c)	(d)	(e)
	Number	Percent of total	Number	Percent of total mergers in size class (c)/(a)	As percent of total conglomerate mergers (c)/665
1–4.9	609	19.9	122	20.0	18.3
5–9.9	510	16.0	98	19.2	14.7
10–24.9	717	22.5	153	21.3	23.0
25–49.9	457	14.4	88	19.3	13.2
50 and over	889	27.9	204	22.9	30.7
TOTALS	3,182	100.0	665	20.9	100.0

[a] Detail may not add to totals because of rounding.
SOURCE: Derived from Table 11.

in the $10 million-and-more grouping, 66.9 percent of all conglomerate mergers were found in that group. And in the largest group ($50 million and over) 22.9 percent of the mergers were conglomerate, the highest percentage for any size class. Moreover, 30.7 percent of all conglomerate mergers occurred within this group, but only 27.9 percent of all mergers.

These data suggest a possible relationship between size of the acquiring firm and number of conglomerate mergers. However, at present they do not permit an inference of a substantial difference in the percentage of conglomerate mergers by size of the firm. The 30.7 percent of conglomerate mergers consummated by the largest firms cannot be considered as substantially greater than the 27.9 percent of all consummated by that size class. Nor can the other differences indicated be construed as conclusive. Given the limited data available, we can conclude only that large firms tend to merge more than others, and that conglomerate mergers account for at least a proportionate share of merger activity in all size classes.

If adequate data were available, it would be interesting to investigate the null hypothesis that there is no relationship between size of acquiring firm and number of conglomerate mergers. Another FTC finding suggests the possible rejection of this null hypothesis, and hence support for the relationship. The Commission found an association between large *acquired* firms and conglomerate mergers, and noted that the advantages of diversification conferred upon the acquiring firm were more frequent in acquisitions of large or medium-size properties than in acquisitions of small-size properties.[22] Since only a large firm usually can undertake a large acquisition, we have additional support for the possible relationship between size of acquiring firm and number of conglomerate mergers.

---

[22] *Ibid.*, p. 8.

SUMMARY

The level of classification of census data is a critical factor in revealing the extent of diversification in the economy. If classifications blur the non-substitutability of various products by grouping them under common headings, they understate the true magnitude of diversification. In spite of grouping together some independently demanded products, the census data pointedly reveal the significance of diversification. In a relatively broad classification, multi-industry companies accounted for 44.4 percent of the total business and industry employment in 1958. And the recent rapid growth of multi-industry companies is evident in their 59 percent increase between 1954 and 1958.

Between 1954 and 1958, decreased industry specialization occurred primarily through gains in "secondary" industry activities relative to lesser gains in primary activities. At the 4-digit classification level, 41 percent of all manufacturing employment was accounted for by industries with specialization ratios of less than 75 percent. The extent of diversification is even more clearly seen at the 5-digit level. Among the largest 1,000 manufacturing companies, fewer than 5 percent confined themselves to a single 5-digit product class and only 21 percent to four or fewer classes.

Within the over-all upward trend in mergers since the late forties, manufacturing has accounted for the bulk of all mergers. About two-thirds of the industrial mergers for 1946–1961 were consummated by large firms. Mergers having only conglomerate elements constituted 20 to 30 percent of all mergers between 1940 and 1954. A 30 percent conglomerate-to-total ratio was recorded in 1954, and there is good reason to suppose the ratio has continued to maintain at least that level. If partly conglomerate mergers are also considered, conglomerate activity becomes very significant.

The data suggested, in terms of mergers having solely conglomerate elements, that there may possibly be a greater tendency for "large" firms to effect them than for smaller firms. However, the existence of any significant relationship between size of the acquiring firm and number of conglomerate mergers can be ascertained only with additional empirical investigations. The data at hand do permit at least the conclusion that conglomerate mergers have maintained at the minimum a proportionately equal share of total merger activity as classified by size of the acquiring firm.

Chapter III

THE LEGISLATIVE
HISTORY OF
CONGLOMERATE MERGERS

THE implications of conglomerate mergers for competition can be understood only if we first understand precisely what the Congress meant by the term "conglomerate mergers." To date, there has been no adequate analysis of the Congressional intent regarding conglomerate mergers, particularly as it is evident in the history of the 1950 Amendment of Section 7 of the Clayton Act. The discussion here will not go into detail regarding the background and specific amendment efforts of the several Section 7 issues that received far more attention than did conglomerate mergers, but will consider those matters only insofar as they are relevant to the rise of interest in and the form of the eventual inclusion of conglomerates in the Amendment.[1]

THE EVOLUTION OF THE 1950 AMENDMENT

Purpose and Economic Background of the Clayton Act

The great merger movement that began at the end of the nineteenth century and extended through 1907 raised many serious issues concerning free enterprise capitalism. The merger section of the 1914 Act established a basic, albeit in-

---

[1] Two works that describe the general history of the 1950 Amendment are David D. Martin, *Mergers and the Clayton Act* (Berkeley: University of California Press, 1959), and "Section 7 of the Clayton Act: A Legislative History," *Columbia Law Review*, LII (June, 1952). Neither deals extensively with the conglomerate merger aspects of the Amendment, however.

complete, public philosophy regarding consolidation of economic power.[2]

At the time of the passage of the Clayton Act, most mergers were achieved by purchase of stock rather than by purchase of assets. Typically, one corporation bought controlling stock in a competitive corporation.[3] It was easier to purchase stock than assets, especially by holding companies, which usually would merely exchange their stock for that of a company to be absorbed. This merger movement as a whole, and the stock-exchange aspect in particular, encouraged stock "watering." Often the huge consolidations were put together by promoters who issued stock largely in order to pay off the owners of the acquired companies.[4]

Because corporate acquisitions typically took the form of stock purchases, there was relatively little immediate need in 1914 for Section 7 to deal with asset acquisitions. The omission of assets in the 1914 Act should not be construed, however, as indicating a Congressional lack of concern regarding economic concentration. At the time, stock acquisitions were the predominant form of merger. Indeed, the intent of Congress is clearly evident in the report accompanying the bill issued by the Committee of the Judiciary of the U.S. Senate.[5]

The relevant content of that report was pointed out during floor debate on the more recent Celler Bill. Representative (Mrs.) Douglas quoted the 1914 intent-of-Congress statement:

> Broadly stated, the bill, in its treatments of unlawful restraints and monopolies, seeks to prohibit and make unlawful certain trade practices, which, as a rule, singly and in themselves, are

---

[2] U.S., Federal Trade Commission, *Report on Corporate Mergers and Acquisitions* (Washington: U.S. Government Printing Office, 1955), p. 145.

[3] *Ibid.*

[4] U.S., Congress, House, Committee on the Judiciary, *Amending An Act Approved October 15, 1914*, 81st Congress, 1st Sess., 1949, House Report 1191 to accompany H.R. 2734, p. 4.

[5] See U.S., Congress, Senate, Committee on the Judiciary, 63rd Cong., 2d Sess., July 22, 1914, S. Rept. 698 to accompany H.R. 15657, p. 1.

not covered by the act of July 2, 1890 [Sherman Act], or other existing antitrust acts and thus, by making these practices illegal, to arrest the creation of trusts, conspiracies, and monopolies in their incipiency and before consummation.[6]

Decisions emasculating the 1914 Act

The United States Supreme Court in 1926 rendered a single decision covering three Section 7 cases it had considered simultaneously.[7] The Court declared that, if an acquiring corporation through its stock purchases secured title to the physical assets of the acquired corporation before the Federal Trade Commission issued its complaint, the Commission was powerless to order divestiture of the assets. In 1934 the Supreme Court further extended the law respecting acquisitions of stock control subsequently converted into outright purchases of assets, holding that, if an acquiring corporation secured title to the physical assets of a corporation whose stock it had acquired before the FTC issued its final order, the Commission lacked the power to direct divestiture of the physical assets even though the acquisition of stock control may have fallen within the prohibition of Section 7 of the Clayton Act.[8]

SECTION 7 AMENDMENT EFFORTS

Assets Loophole: Primary Focus

In view of the emasculating Supreme Court decisions, amendments to remedy the assets loophole were soon forthcoming. Beginning in 1927, the Federal Trade Commission itself annually set forth amendment proposals. The Temporary National Economic Committee in its 1941 final report proposed an even more stringent amendment to Section 7 not

---

[6] U.S., Congressional Record, 81st Cong., 1st Sess., 1949, XCV, Part 9, 11500.

[7] *Federal Trade Commission v. Western Meat Co.*; *Thatcher Manufacturing Co. v. Federal Trade Commission*; and *Swift and Co. v. Federal Trade Commission* (272 U.S. 554).

[8] *Arrow-Hart and Hegeman Electric Co. v. Federal Trade Commission* (291 U.S. 587).

only joining the FTC in an effort to eliminate the assets loophole in mergers between competing corporations but also recommending a requirement of FTC approval in advance of consummation for all mergers above a given size.

Advocates of tightening antimerger policy argued that the assets loophole was fostering centralization of economic and political power. Comments by Senator O'Mahoney, chairman of the T.N.E.C. and author of one of the early amendment bills, typify the many statements expressing fear of centralization. In 1945, for example, the Senator said:

> If we do not take the alternative presented by this bill, of preventing mergers, then we will be confronted with the choice of having the economic life of the country managed by private groups or by public groups; but it is my judgment that the people will turn to public groups, because that is what they have been doing.[9]

Unmentioned in this statement, but noted explicitly and frequently throughout the hearings on the many bills to amend Section 7, was awareness that the rise of cartels—in Germany for example—apparently enhanced the possibility of political dominance by a narrow economic segment of the nation. Many cited a similar pattern of apparent economic, then political domination, in Japan. There were frequent references also to the ascendancy of the Labour party in post-World War II England and to its nationalization drive. The central theme of the argument was that a country could not hope to prevent a steady trend toward centralized government unless it prevented concentration of economic power; maintenance of decentralized government required preservation of competitive free enterprise in the states.[10]

Testifying during the Celler Bill hearings in 1949, Herbert A. Bergson, Chief of the Antitrust Division of the Department of Justice, typified the administrative agencies' focus on the Section 7 loophole:

---

[9] U.S., Congress, House, Subcommittee of the Committee on the Judiciary, *Hearings on H.R. 2357* 79th Cong., 1st Sess., 1945, p. 16.

[10] *Ibid.* and *passim.*

As the Clayton Act now reads, it is powerless to meet this problem. H.R. 2734 (Celler) is designed to correct the situation by amending section 7 to achieve the purpose which was back of the original enactment.

Section 7 of the Clayton Act was designed to prevent the acquisition by one corporation of the stock of competing corporations where the result would be substantially to lessen competition.

In 1914, when the Act was passed, it was thought that the Sherman Act was adequate to meet the problems arising in connection with the acquisition of assets.

Accordingly the Clayton Act was directed only to stock acquisitions. Since that time, however, court decisions have limited the application of the Sherman Act in this field, with the result that neither the Clayton Act as it now reads nor Sherman Act as it has been interpreted is adequate to deal with the problem of asset acquisitions.

The latest decision of the Supreme Court on the subject, *United States* v. *Columbia Steel Co.* [334 U.S. 495 (1948)], documents the need for more effective legislation if the objective which Congress had in mind when it passed the Clayton Act back in 1914 is to be achieved.[11]

At present, Section 7 of the Clayton Act does not prevent the acquisition of assets, nor does it provide authority for the F.T.C. to order divestiture of assets acquired as a result of illegal acquisitions of stock.[12]

---

[11] To be sure, the intent of Congress in 1914 is variously interpreted. Gilbert H. Montague, a practicing antitrust lawyer, argued adamantly that the intent was merely to prevent "overnight" acquisitions of stock and intentionally excluded asset acquisitions from the coverage of the Act. His reasoning is based on close personal contact with Mr. Brandeis (later Justice Brandeis), who had a great deal to do with the phraseology of Section 7 of the 1914 Act. According to Montague, "It is a calumny on Congress to suggest that there was any oversight at that time. They intended it just as it is, and this talk about a loophole and an oversight is just not so." U.S., Congress, House, Subcommittee of the Committee on the Judiciary, *Hearings on H.R. 2734*, 81st Cong., 1st Sess., 1949, p. 42. However, for the opposite and prevailing opinion see, for example, the testimony of Senator O'Mahoney citing the minority opinions (Brandeis *included*) of the Supreme Court in the two emasculating decisions. U.S., Congress, Senate, Subcommittee of the Committee on the Judiciary, *Hearing on H.R. 2734*, 81st Cong., 1st and 2d Sess., 1949–1950, pp. 9–10.

[12] U.S., Congress, House, *Hearings on H.R. 2734*, pp. 27–28.

The central attention commanded by the assets loophole in these amendment efforts is evident in the Senate and House reports accompanying the 1950 amendment—as, for example, in the Senate Judiciary Committee statement that the failure of the 1914 Act to prohibit direct purchase of assets has made "inconsistent and paradoxical . . . the overall effect of existing law."[13]

In total, 21 separate bills to amend Section 7 were introduced in Congress between 1927 and 1949. The principal amendment efforts were made subsequent to the T.N.E.C. final recommendation of 1941. Sixteen amendment bills were introduced from 1943 to 1949. The amendment activity culminated in the Celler-Kefauver Act of December 29, 1950 (64 U.S.C.A. 1125).

Conglomerate Mergers

One of the earliest legislative incidents germane to conglomerate mergers is an exhibit contained in a House of Representatives report on a 1946 bill to amend Section 7. Although the focus of that bill was solely on horizontal mergers, among the various exhibits presented to show the high frequency of mergers effected by purchase of assets and resulting in superconcentration, some examples revealed the extent to which diversified firms were involved.[14] It was not until the following year, however, that the issues of diversification began to achieve explicit attention.

FTC Report, 1947.—The Federal Trade Commission on March 7, 1947 submitted to Congress *The Present Trend of Corporate Mergers and Acquisitions*, a report pointing out the need for plugging the assets loophole by showing the number of acquisitions of smaller companies by larger ones

---

[13] U.S., Congress, Senate, Committee on the Judiciary, *Amending an Act Approved October 15, 1914*, 81st Cong., 2d Sess., 1950, S. Rept. 1775 to accompany H.R. 2734, p. 2.

[14] U.S., Congress, House, Committee on the Judiciary, *Amending Sections 7 and 11 of the Clayton Act*, 79th Cong., 2d Sess., 1940, H. Rept. 1820 to accompany H.R. 5535.

in 1940–1946.[15] Three of the report's twenty-three pages presented a breakdown of mergers by types. This breakdown is highly significant. The Commission characterized 22 percent of the 1940–1946 mergers as conglomerate, *i.e.*, mergers "in which there is no discernible relationship in the nature of business between the purchasing and the acquired firms."[16]

Two paragraphs of the report suggested the nature and possible effects of conglomerate mergers. It is of interest to note the intensity of feeling in those paragraphs:

> The traditional rationalizations for merger are less applicable to this type of acquisition . . . than to the horizontal and vertical types because of the great difficulty in obtaining thereby any important efficiencies of production and distribution.
>
> Perhaps the most important danger . . . inherent in these conglomerate organizations is the economic power which they can wield over a large number of different industries. Threatened with competition in any one of its fields of enterprise, the conglomerate corporation may sell below cost or may use other unfair methods in that field, absorbing its losses through excessive profits made in its other lines of activity, all rationalized in the name of "meeting competition." The conglomerate corporation is thus in a position to strike out with great force against small business in a variety of . . . industries. There are few greater dangers to small business today than the continued growth of the conglomerate corporations.[17]

The report conjectured that conglomerate acquisitions would tend to increase under the continuing postwar pressure on many large corporations to seek employment for their large accumulations of profits.[18]

House of Representatives Bill 515.—Hearings on Repre-

---

[15] U.S., Congress, *The Present Trend of Corporate Mergers and Acquisitions*, Document 17, 80th Cong., 1st Sess., 1947.

[16] *Ibid.*, p. 12.

[17] *Ibid.*, pp. 12–13.

[18] *Ibid.*, p. 14.

sentative Kefauver's bill, H.R. 515, began in March, 1947. In view of the FTC's keen interest in the Section 7 amendment, the submission of the pointed FTC report discussed above only twelve days before the beginning of the hearings was probably not entirely fortuitous. Indeed, in his opening remarks Kefauver entered the FTC report in the record,[19] although dealing only with the cause and effects of the assets loophole generally and not mentioning conglomerate mergers specifically. Similarly, R. E. Freer of the FTC treated the merger problem as a unit. Conglomerate mergers received no explicit attention in the hearings. However, their eventual inclusion was aided by the elimination of the "acquiring-acquired" clause of Section 7. This clause had served to focus Section 7 only on the substantial lessening of competition between the acquiring and the acquired companies. To be sure, no merger between two companies "lessens competition" between them—that is, makes for *less competition*; such a merger simply and completely eliminates competition between them. The courts had tended to apply a Sherman Act ("rule of reason") test and in effect to render the section identical to the 1890 Act.[20] Thus, although originally intending to halt at once acquisitions insufficient to fall within the scope of the Sherman Act, the Clayton Act was by judicial interpretation reconstrued as, at best, a substitute for the 1890 Act. It was primarily Representative Clifford Case who perceptively —and successfully—sought a shift of focus from a test of competition between acquiring and acquired firms to a broader test of the *effect* of the merger. Case's questioning resulted in modification of the original wording achieving a compromise between the extremes of the monopoly test and complete prohibition of mergers between competitors; the effect of the merger "in any line of commerce or in any section, com-

---

[19] U.S., Congress, House, Subcommittee of the Committee on the Judiciary, *Hearings on H.R. 515*, 80th Cong., 1st Sess., 1947, p. 5.

[20] It was the opinion of William T. Kelley, chief counsel of the FTC, that the International Shoe Co. case exemplified the Supreme Court's rule-of-reason construction. *International Shoe Co.* v. *F.T.C.* (280 U.S. 291). See Kelley's comments, *Hearings*, p. 119.

munity, or trade area"[21] became the focal criterion.

This shift of the Section 7 test in regard to non-horizontal mergers was significant. The concern with effects *beyond* the parties to the merger paved the way for a logical interest in the effects of vertical and conglomerate mergers as well. Fruits of this labor were borne in House of Representatives Report 596 accompanying H.R. Bill 3736 (originally Kefauver Bill H.R. 515). Although without mentioning conglomerate or vertical acquisitions, this report served to eliminate the more restrictive test as to reduction of competition between acquiring and acquired companies and substituted a standard whereby "in any line of commerce in any section of the country, the effect of such acquisition may be to substantially lessen competition."[22] The bill failed to get a rule from the Rules Committee, but this elimination of the "Clayton Act test" was achieved in the eventual Section 7 bill. No single change in the history of amendment efforts was more instrumental in allowing for inclusion of conglomerate mergers than this modification. To have concentrated solely on the assets loophole would have been insufficient.

FTC Report, 1948.—In 1948 the FTC stepped up the pace of its crusade for amendment of Section 7 by publishing *The Merger Movement: A Summary Report*. This 134-page document represented almost a quarter-century of Commission efforts in this area. The primary focus continued to be on plugging the assets loophole. But now, in pressing the attack on the loophole, the report divided mergers into various categories and presented typical examples in each. Three subgroups of vertical acquisitions were discussed—forward, backward, and two-way; horizontal mergers were also divided into three subgroups—direct, substitute products, and chain (or series) acquisitions of firms making similar products for

---

[21] *Ibid.*, p. 118. See pages 22, 37, 52–54, 81, 119 for some of Representative Case's line of inquiry, and pages 118–119 for FTC Counsel's recommendation.

[22] U.S., Congress, House, Committee on the Judiciary, *Amending Section 7 and 11 of the Clayton Act*, 80th Cong., 1st Sess., 1947, H. Rept. 596 to accompany H.R. 3736, p. 5.

local market consumption. The report noted the impossibility of classifying conglomerate acquisitions into meaningful subgroups since "practically every conglomerate action is a case by itself."[23]

The report contained four pages on conglomerate mergers, observing that there is less economic justification for this form than for other patterns of growth. For example, conglomerate acquisitions do not engender augmentation of production skills and know-how, as horizontal acquisitions often do. Economies like those which may occur in vertical mergers by improved flow of materials through production stages generally are not to be found in conglomerate mergers. The report declared that it was not disallowing any possibility of economies in conglomerate acquisitions, but that, with dissimilar economic activities and no technological relationship, economies can be achieved only with great difficulty or are minimal at best.[24] Indeed, the definition of conglomerate mergers in this 1948 report referred to this factor, substituting the concept of "little or no discernible relation"[25] for the 1947 report's "no discernible relationship."[26] By allowing for the possibility of some economic relationship between parties to a merger, the 1948 report could speak of possible minimal economies. The implications of this change of definition were to become more fully evident by 1950.

In the 1948 report, the Commission also repeated a warning that it had issued before—a warning that arose time and again in the history of Section 7 amendments efforts. Implicitly relevant to conglomerate acquisitions, this warning evinced a general concern about economic concentration and its political and social results:

> No great stretch of the imagination is required to foresee that if nothing is done to check the growth in concentration

---

[23] U.S., Federal Trade Commission, *The Merger Movement, A Summary Report* (Washington: U.S. Government Printing Office, 1948), pp. 31–32.
[24] *Ibid.*, pp. 59–60.
[25] *Ibid.*, p. 59
[26] *The Present Trend of Corporate Mergers and Acquisitions*, p. 12.

either the giant corporations will ultimately take over the country, or the Government will be impelled to step in and impose some form of direct regulation in the public interest. In either event, collectivism will have triumphed over free enterprise, and the theory of competition will have been relegated to limbo of well-intentioned but ineffective ideals.[27]

House of Representatives Bill 2734.—The impact of the hearings on the Kefauver Bill (H.R. 515) in the 80th Congress was seen in the 81st Congress. In the latter Congress three bills to amend Section 7 were introduced by Representatives Jackson, Hobbs, and Celler, each omitting the Clayton Act's "acquiring-acquired" test. The way was thus cleared for inclusion of conglomerate mergers. Hearings were held on the Celler Bill (H.R. 2734), to which the Jackson and Hobbs bills were essentially similar.[28]

It is instructive in understanding the climate of feeling during the hearings to view the statements of two of the most staunch proponents of amending Section 7, Senator Kefauver and Representative Celler. At the opening of the hearings, Kefauver said:

> I feel, gentlemen, that if our democracy is going to survive in this country, we must keep competition, and we must see to it that the basic materials and resources of the country are available to any little fellow who wants to go into business. . . . When people lose their economic freedom, they lose their political freedom.
>
> I do want to urge, while there is still time to save our free economy, before we reach the point of concentration where we are going to have a demand for state control of these basic industries, in order to preserve our free-enterprise system where every person and small corporation can have an opportunity of competing, that this committee exercise its good judgement and plug this loophole in Sec. 7 of the Clayton

---

[27] *The Merger Movement, A Summary Report*, p. 68.
[28] For comparisons of the various bills introduced in the 81st Congress, 1st Session, see U.S., Congress, House, Subcommittee of the Committee on the Judiciary, *Hearings on H.R. 2734*, 81st Cong., 1st Sess., 1949, pp. 1–11.

Act and carry out the apparent intent of Congress when it
passed the Act in 1914. . . . Actually, this is protection for the
very big businesses as well, because, if we do not have this,
big businesses are not going to be privately owned in the
years to come.[29]

In a similar vein, Celler testified:

> Our greatness as a Nation rises or falls as the dignity and
> independence of the individual, the small-business man, the
> mechanic, the small shop-keeper, and so on, contracts or ex-
> pands.
>
> In other words, the worth of the individual is the worth of
> the Nation; no more no less. That which strengthens the
> individual bolsters the Nation; that which dwarfs the individ-
> ual belittles the Nation.
>
> The individual and small-business man cannot flower
> amidst the weeds of monopoly. Great masses of economic
> power and monopoly stunt the growth of the individual enter-
> prise and kills individual ambition and individual dignity.
>
> I do not want the impression to prevail from any statement I
> made that bigness is in and of itself an evil. It is what big
> business can do that may be mischievous. Our economy has
> been so developed over the years that big business may be
> essential if managed properly and in due interest of the pub-
> lic. But we also need small business and we dare not let a
> system develop that would blot out small business.[30]

Study of Monopoly Power

After the hearings on H.R. 2734 (which were completed in
one day, May 18, 1949) and before the reporting out of the
bill by the full House Committee on the Judiciary, a Subcommittee of the House Committee on the Judiciary began
a separate study on monopoly power and held hearings in
July-August, 1949. During the monopoly hearings, a relatively large amount of testimony was given about conglomerates.

---

[29] *Ibid.*, pp. 12–13.
[30] *Ibid.*, pp. 14–16.

This testimony undoubtedly influenced the substance and emphasis of the House Report on the Celler Bill.

On July 20, 1949, Dr. John M. Blair, Chief, Division of Economics, Bureau of Industrial Economics, Federal Trade Commission, spoke about conglomerate mergers:

> There is another type, the conglomerate acquisition . . . [in which the] type of business of the acquiring firm is only distantly, if at all, related to the business of the acquired firm. In this respect it differs from the other types of acquisitions where there exists some logical relationship between the business of the acquiring firm and the acquired firm. . . .
>
> The Commission feels that the conglomerate type of acquisition is one which is peculiarly dangerous to small business. A company that is so diversified is in a position to strike out with great force against any smaller company which may seek to compete with it in any one of the variety of fields in which it is engaged and, of course, it is able to make up whatever losses that are incurred in the competitive war with its profits secured in the other fields in which it is engaged.[31]

Several days later, Professor Walter Adams of Michigan State College testified:

> Conglomerate size is a problem in a competitive system, because it gives the large firm undue power as a buyer of materials, energy, transportation, credit, and labor. Such firms enjoy a special advantage in litigation, politics, public relations, and finance . . . they can afford to maintain some powerful lobbies in Washington. . . . The conglomerate firm, by virtue of its diversification, can discipline or destroy its more specialized competitors.[32]

In dialogue with a witness, Celler questioned the economic justification of conglomerate mergers. Speaking about a conglomerate's competitive strength, Celler observed:

---

[31] U.S., Congress, House, Subcommittee of the Committee on the Judiciary, *Hearings on Study of Monopoly Power*, 81st Cong., 1st Sess., 1949, Serial No. 14, Part 1, pp. 219–220.

[32] *Ibid.*, pp. 349–350.

Yes, but it does not follow that it betters the race for survival; that, if somebody makes cheese, he must go out and control the market for chalk. One has got nothing to do with the
other.

What, for example, has the manufacturer of soap to do with
the importation and distribution of teas, as in the case of
Lever Bros.? They do not have to survive in the soap business
only if they acquire a strangle hold on the importation and
the distribution of tea.

The witness, F. I. Raymond, author of *The Limitist*, com-
mented as follows on why companies might be prompted to
make conglomerate acquisitions: "I think that our taxing
system has had a good deal to do with forcing corporations
who had surpluses to use those surpluses for the purchase of
any company that was available to them."[33]

Professor Philip C. Newman of Pennsylvania State College
offered an explanation of why large conglomerates arise
and underscored the cumulative concentrating processes
involved:

They [the Unilever Combine] have taken over many industries which are not directly related to the initial manufacturing process, because, if I may say so, Sir, there are two stages
of a combine's growth. The first is where it integrates vertically and takes over the raw materials which it needs for its
end products right down the line, vertical integration; and
then, later, where they integrate horizontally, where they
have a very extensive sales organization, and they think the
sales organization is not moving at capacity, and then you get
a lot of unrelated products, because they start taking over
something which the salesmen can carry also, in addition to
the first products of the firm, and then they start taking over
the factory of the products which the salesmen are carrying,
and before you know it, they are in a lot of fields which have
no relation to the initial product.[34]

But I think there is danger in this diversification because the

---

[33] *Ibid.*, Parts 2-A, 2-B, p. 305.
[34] *Ibid.*, p. 419.

cumulative process of key concentration goes on, and the minute you diversify there is another field in which you are going to start acquiring suppliers and sources of raw materials, and again and again and again. All the cats have kittens, and the kittens become big, and you have more kittens, and the next thing you know diversification becomes integration; integration becomes diversification, and then you have a web that looks like this.[35]

What should public policy be in regard to conglomerate concentration? This perplexing question was posed by various congressmen, including Celler:

How far should government, the people, allow that kind of concentration, which for want of a better name we call conglomerate concentration, to proceed? . . . If no brakes are placed on it, we are going to have, are we not, a few dominating companies like General Motors, which in effect is a holding company, purely an investment holding company? . . . Is not the consumer, which is part of the public, affected by the fact that the General Motors Corporation becomes sort of a collectivist corporation? . . . You get to a point where it is so large that it affects the lives and happiness of so many people, that as a matter of fact, you could not let it fail.[36]

Comments about the antisocial nature of conglomerates usually took one of two courses: the conglomerate was seen either as a competitive staying power superior to that of the small, single-product firm or as a large, economic agglomeration approaching economic collectivism. The testimony suggested that the primary concern of the legislators was the economic-concentration aspect of conglomerates. On the other hand the majority of the economists' testimony stressed the superior-market-power aspect. Economic concentration was singularly stressed by the lawmakers, and it alone appeared to serve as sufficient motivation for legislation to curb conglomerate mergers. Seemingly preoccupied with the con-

---

[35] *Ibid.*, p. 434.
[36] *Ibid.*, p. 636.

centration aspects, the appropriate Congressional committees never requested a rigorous analysis of the economic effects a conglomerate can produce in the markets.

Since Congress was primarily concerned with concentration, it is understandable that the economic effects that "may substantially lessen competition or tend to create a monopoly" were never to receive a thorough analytical airing. And this lack of analysis extended also to the behavior of conglomerates that produces such effects, and indeed also to those structural determinants that *a priori* imply the possibility of the effects.

House of Representatives Report 1191.—H.R. Report 1191 explicitly incorporated conglomerate mergers in H.R. 2734. With the broad intent of amending Section 7 so as to prohibit the acquisition of assets as well as stock of any corporation under the jurisdiction of the FTC if the effect would tend "substantially to lessen competition, or tend to create a monopoly," the bill substituted "in any line of commerce in any section of the country" for the language of the original Section 7 "acquiring-acquired" test.[37]

The report stated that the amending legislation was not intended to duplicate existing legislation, but to focus on the cumulative effects of a series of stock or asset acquisitions that would be sufficient to constitute control of the market. Thus the bill was intended to permit intervention in just such a cumulative process when the acquisition would tend to produce a significant reduction in the vigor of the competition —even though the effect would be insufficient to amount to a combination in restraint of trade, creation of a monopoly, or an attempt to monopolize, i.e., acts proscribed under the Sherman Act.[38]

Given the bill's standards—whether the merger may substantially lessen competition or tend to create a monopoly—

---

[37] U.S., Congress, House, Committee on the Judiciary, *Amending an Act Approved October 15, 1914*, 81st Cong., 1st Sess., 1949, H. Rept. 1191 to accompany H.R. 2734, pp. 5–6.

[38] *Ibid.*, p. 8.

the administrative agencies would not have to inquire, as they do under the Sherman Act, into the motive for a merger, or to prove that the acquiring firm had engaged in unethical or predatory actions, or to show that as a result of a merger the acquiring firm had already obtained a degree of control sufficient to destroy or exclude competitors or fix prices.[39] Moreover, the test of substantial lessening of competition or tending to create a monopoly was intended to protect competition in each line of commerce in each section of the country, and not merely where the specified effect may appear in a nation-wide or industry-wide scale.[40]

The report also dealt with actions which might be undertaken in order to avoid evasion of its central purpose. The amending language covered not only the purchase of assets or stock, but any other method of acquisition, such as lease of assets or indirect acquisitions through a subsidiary or affiliate or otherwise.[41]

In contradistinction to the "strong" moves, however, the report defined conglomerate acquisitions in the narrower of the two versions mentioned earlier.[42] It defined conglomerate acquisitions simply as those in which there is "no discernible relationship in the nature of business between the acquiring and acquired firms."[43]

House Debate and Action.—The comments relevant to conglomerate mergers made during floor debate can be divided into two parts: data on concentration and specific mention of conglomerate mergers.

In giving the background of his bill, Representative Celler stated that of the three million business units in the United States only 445 or .125 percent of all corporations own 51 percent of the nation's gross assets. Because of the loophole, the years 1940–1947 saw more than 2,500 independent con-

---

[39] *Ibid.*
[40] *Ibid.*, pp. 8–9.
[41] *Ibid.*
[42] *The Present Trend of Corporate Mergers and Acquisitions.*
[43] *Ibid.*, p. 11.

cerns disappear through merger. Their assets, 5.2 billion dollars, comprised 5.5 percent of the total assets of all manufacturing corporations. He cited additional FTC statistics to the effect that by 1949, 250 firms controlled two-thirds of the industrial facilities of the country, whereas a decade earlier 15,000 companies controlled the same percentage. These 250 concerns bought up 70 percent of the government-built war plants.[44]

Celler stated that four companies handled 64 percent of the steel business in the country; four made 82 percent of the copper sales; two accounted for 90 percent of aluminum production; three had 85 percent of the auto business; two made 80 percent of the electric lamp sales; four held 75 percent of the electric refrigerator business; two had 80 percent of the glass business; and four accounted for 90 percent of the cigarette sales. These were declared to be typical examples of the concentration to be found in individual industries.

Citing 1937 T.N.E.C. findings, Celler also declared that one-third of the total value of all manufactured products were produced under conditions in which the leading four producers of each product supplied between 75 and 100 percent of the total value. Furthermore, 37 percent of the total value of all manufactured products was accounted for by the largest four producers of each product controlling more than 50 percent of that product's total value.[45] He continued:

> It is very difficult now for small business to compete against the financial, purchasing, and advertising power of the mammoth corporations. . . . Bigness does not mean efficiency, a better product, or lower prices. Buying raw materials or parts by the combines at lower prices is often a matter of sheer power. Suppliers are often compelled to accept what huge companies choose to pay. Volume of advertising is large in amount and impact but low in proportion to enormous sales.

---

[44] U.S., *Congressional Record*, 81st Cong., 1st Sess., 1949, XCV, Part 9, 11485.
[45] *Ibid.*, 11485–11486.

Great wealth and credit are frequently matters of favor or accident or sheer power.[46]

In the floor debate, all of which took place on August 15, 1949, discussion of conglomerate mergers was sparse. Representative Boggs of Louisiana mentioned them very briefly but significantly:

> A third avenue of expansion—and this is one of the most detrimental movements to a free enterprise economy—is the conglomerate acquisition. This is the type which carries the activities of the giant corporations into all sorts of fields, often completely unrelated to their normal operations. In times such as these, when big corporations have such huge quantities of funds,[47] they are constantly looking around for new kinds of businesses to enter. By this process they build up huge business enterprises which enable them to play one type of business against another in order to drive out competition.[48]

In view of the historic attitude of the House Rules Committee towards Section 7 bills, Celler moved to suspend the rules and pass the bill. This action allowed only limited floor debate and required two-thirds affirmative vote. At the end of the August 15 floor debate, the House, voting 223 yeas, 92 nays, and 117 not voting, passed the bill.[49]

Senate Action on H.R. 2734

The Senate Committee on the Judiciary reported out H.R. 2734 with but minor changes. Senate Report 1775 did not mention conglomerate mergers explicitly, but the Senate Judiciary Committee implicitly recognized them by recommending passage of H.R. 2734. On December 13, 1950, the Senate

---

[46] *Ibid.*, 11486.
[47] Rep. Boggs had mentioned previously that the large corporations had emerged from the war with immense reserves of funds; *viz.*, as of June, 1947, the 78 largest corporations possessed $10 billion of highly liquid net working capital, which was sufficient, he said, to purchase the assets of nearly 90 percent of all manufacturing corporations.
[48] *Ibid.*, 11496.
[49] *Ibid.*, 11507.

passed H.R. 2734 with minor amendments. The vote was 55 yeas to 22 nays, with 19 not voting.[50] President Truman signed the bill on December 29, 1950.[51]

EXAMPLES OF CONGLOMERATE MERGERS IN THE
LEGISLATIVE HISTORY OF THE AMENDMENT

A number of examples of conglomerate mergers were presented in several of the hearings and studies cited above. A changing conception of these mergers is evident from the examples offered during the period leading to the 1950 amendment.

1947 FTC Report

The Federal Trade Commission presented three examples of conglomerate mergers in its 1947 report: the Maytag Washing Machine Co. purchase of a manufacture of chicken brooders, the American Type Founders, Inc. purchase of a manufacture of high-fidelity radio sets and chromium and plastic furniture, and the merger of Detrola Corporation (radios and radio parts) with International Machine Tool Co.[52] In each instance the acquired firm marketed a substantially different line of products from that of the acquiring firm.

1948 FTC Report

From 1940 to approximately 1948, conglomerate acquisitions of various types occurred in all manufacturing, but particularly in the machinery, food, petroleum, and drug industries. In its 1948 report, the FTC listed several examples of conglomerate acquisitions—examples for the most part of a higher node commonality than the three in its 1947 report. The examples cited in the 1948 report included acquisitions by machinery manufacturers: the purchase of a can-machinery

---

[50] U.S., *Congressional Record*, 81st Cong., 2d Sess., 1950, XCVI, Part 12, 16508. See *Ibid.*, 16574, concerning the House of Representatives' accepting the Senate amendments.

[51] *Ibid.*, 17138.

[52] *The Present Trend of Corporate Mergers and Acquisitions*, p. 12.

firm by a diesel-engine manufacturer (Modern Can Machinery Co. and Imperial Diesel Engine Co.); the acquisition of a paper-bottle company by a large manufacturer of precision parts for aircraft, diesels, and automobiles (Ex-Cell-O Corp. bought American Paper Bottle Co.); the merger of a leading vacuum-cleaner manufacturer with an oil-burner firm (Eureka Vacuum Cleaner Co. and Williams Oil-O-Matic Heating Corp.).

The report also cited the postwar diversification of aircraft producers into such fields as movie equipment, radio, agricultural equipment, and burial-casket manufacture. It specifically noted the Curtiss-Wright purchase of Victor Animatograph Corp., the Avco Corp. acquisition of the radio, household equipment, and radio-station business of Crosley Corp., as well as of New Idea, Inc., a farm-implement company; and Solar Aircraft's purchase of the Hubbard Casket Manufacturing Co.

In food production, the Commission reported the purchase by Creameries of America, Inc. (wholesale and retail milk distribution in the Western States and hay, grain, and feed distribution in the Hawaiian Islands) of the Hawaii Brewing Corp. General Foods broadened its holdings through a number of acquisitions in lines new to General Foods: notably, Bireley's Inc. (processor of citrus-fruit beverages) and Gaines Food Co. (one of the nation's largest producers of dry dog food). Standard Brands also diversified; the company entered the margarine business by purchasing Standard Margarine Co., Inc., one of the three largest producers of margarine in the United States, whose Blue Bonnet line, in turn, made widely diversified products such as salad dressings, peanut butter, sandwich spread, and allied foods.

According to the Commission's report, it was in the drug industry, however, that conglomerate acquisitions were most prevalent. Nearly all leading drug companies had undertaken mergers of all major types: horizontal; vertical, both backward into the production of basic chemicals and forward into the operation of retail chain stores as well as into wholesaling of drug products; and, late in the period covered, conglomerate mergers with a wide variety of manufacturing companies. The case of the American Home Products Co., the FTC said, illustrates the extent of mergers in drugs:

> Since its incorporation (1926), it has acquired no less than 60 formerly independent companies, of which 32 have been purchased since 1940. . . . American Home Products has regularly pointed out to its stockholders that it is following a "continuing policy of expansion and diversification" through purchase and acquisition of other companies.

The report then gave a listing of a few of the best-known brands acquired; Bi-So-Dol, Anacin, Three-in-One Oil, Clapp's Baby Food, Duff's Baking Mix, Chef Boy-Ar-Dee Spaghetti Dinner, etc. The company's 1947 annual report pointed out that 59 percent of the firm's total sales in the preceding year were made by companies acquired since 1936. American Home Products' activities included about 50 subsidiaries and divisions producing approximately 5,000 products.[53]

H.R. Report 1191 and Senate Hearings on H.R. 2734

Curiously enough, whereas the House Hearings on H.R. 2734 did not explicitly mention conglomerate mergers and House Report 1191 on the bill did mention them, the Senate Hearings on H.R. 2734 did include a discussion of conglomerate mergers (primarily by Celler testifying before the Subcommittee) but Senate Report 1775 on the bill did not. When Celler appeared before the Senate Subcommittee of the Committee on the Judiciary on September 21, 1949, he presented three conglomerate merger exhibits taken from H.R. Report 1191. The first showed acquisitions of the Borden Company for the years 1940–1947. In Celler's words:

> From 1940 on they acquired competitors to the left of them and competitors to the right of them. Then you will see how

---

[53] See *The Merger Movement, A Summary Report*, pp. 60–62, for full coverage of these examples.

they moved forward vertically to acquire their customers, like the Texas Milk Products Co., in 1943. . . . Then you see how in conglomerate manner they reached out in other directions unrelated to their basic product, dairy products, milk and ice cream, and they acquired the Farallone Packing Co., packing sardines and fish oil. . . .

Then they acquired Soy Bean Products Co. They acquired pharmaceuticals, and on the other extreme they acquired dog pet foods, and they went into the plastic business. They went into business wholly unrelated to dairy products, milk, ice cream, and so on, and if the loophole is not plugged in our antitrust laws, they will branch out from two soya bean products companies to acquire many other soya bean products companies, and they will branch out from their pharmaceutical company. . . . The same way with plastics. There will be no end to the acquisition of power and influence of the Borden Co. . . .

We offer a third chart that indicates the wide-spread activities of the American Home Products Co. in their conglomerate acquisitions of all kinds of unrelated products. First they bought out competing drug and pharmaceutical houses, you see there, the horizontal acquisitions. Then you see the unrelated acquisitions. They bought out five food specialty houses. They bought out five concerns making waxes and polishes, bought four chemical outfits, bought four dye and paint manufacturing outfits. They bought insecticide outfits, cosmetic outfits. . . .[54]

From these and the preceding mergers cited, the examples of "conglomerate mergers" presented during the period leading up to the 1950 amendment were increasingly of a higher-node-commonality nature. The conception of conglomerate mergers began as an emphasis upon low-node-commonality mergers; however, by 1950, the conception embraced virtually all market-diversification mergers.

---

[54] U.S., Congress, Senate, Subcommittee of the Committee on the Judiciary, *Hearings on H.R. 2734*, 81st Cong., 1st and 2d Sess., 1949–1950, pp. 65–66.

SUMMARY AND CONCLUSIONS

The Meaning of Conglomerate Mergers

Virtually all mergers of corporations—stock acquisitions or asset acquisitions—are covered, subject to certain specifying conditions, by the revised Section 7 of the Clayton Act.[55] As we have seen, the hearings on the Celler-Kefauver Bill, the House report accompanying that bill, and various reports from interested agencies, specified and distinguished the mergers to be covered by the Act as horizontal, vertical, or conglomerate. But the documents provide no precise definition of conglomerate mergers.

The intent of Congress was relatively clear, however. First, all mergers were to be covered. Second, mergers could be classified as those between competing firms and those between noncompeting firms. Third, the latter category included vertically related, non-competing mergers and *non*-vertically related, non-competing mergers. This latter category is the implicit designation of conglomerate mergers.

At the same time, however, Congressmen and interested parties were making statements about conglomerate mergers *per se*. And beginning with the 1947 FTC Report through the H.R. Report 1191, specific examples of conglomerate mergers were given. The earliest examples of conglomerate mergers and definitions focused on mergers of highly dissimilar products. In 1947, for example, the Commission spoke of mergers with "no discernible relationship" between acquiring and acquired firms and cited three examples of seemingly highly disparate activities and products.

---

[55] A description of the statutory standards and complete coverage of the amended Section 7 is not immediately relevant to the present analysis of conglomerate mergers. The description of the Act's coverage appears as Appendix I. The first Section 7 case reviewed by the U.S. Supreme Court was given a comprehensive judicial interpretation. (*Brown Shoe Co., Inc., et al.* v. *U.S.* [370 U.S. 294]. See also Chapter V.) Subsequent Supreme Court reviews of Section 7 cases have further established a body of judicial interpretation.

In its 1948 report, however, the FTC listed many more examples of conglomerate mergers, and the examples cited covered a broader range of node commonality. Some examples in the food and drug fields indicated product-line broadening, others indicated products only distantly related to those of the acquiring firm. Mergers that broaden a product line may indeed be of a high degree of node commonality. Moreover, the definition of conglomerate mergers in this report referred to "little or no discernible relationship" between acquiring and acquired firms. The Commission now suggested that one motivation for conglomerate mergers was the desire to add products that could be marketed with existing sales and personnel and to increase the number of products which could be grouped together in advertisements. By 1948, then, the Commission had developed a more inclusive view of conglomerate mergers than it evinced a year earlier.

Taken literally, the important H.R. Report 1191, which accompanied the amendment bill and presumably attempted to define conglomerate mergers, actually tended to confuse the issue. It reverted to the FTC's strict 1947 definition, but it also included as examples of conglomerate mergers the same high node commonality examples set forth in the FTC's 1948 report.

The foregoing analysis of the record up to and including the passage of the 1950 Amendment leads to two conclusions as to the meaning of "conglomerate mergers." First, one must hold that *all* nonhorizontal, nonvertical mergers are included as conglomerate mergers; both geographic diversification (market extension) and product diversification are included; the record indicates that "no discernible relationship" in the H.R. Report 1191 definition of conglomerate mergers requires only that the products in a merger be noncompeting and non-vertically related; these are the only two definitional criteria for a conglomerate merger.

Second, if conglomerate mergers are identified solely on the basis of absence of horizontal and vertical product relationships, mergers classified as conglomerate may differ greatly in degree of node commonality. They may be characterized by high node commonality or by low node commonality. The array of conglomerate-merger examples offered in the development of the Section 7 Amendment supports this view. The FTC examples in the 1947 report suggest a relatively low degree of node commonality between acquiring and acquired firms. There might be some factor and production commonalities, but the marketing commonalities would appear to be relatively low.

On the other hand, the 1948 examples offered by the Commission include several where the degree of node commonality may well have been relatively high. For instance, several examples in the food field imply commonalities in production, managerial experience, and marketing. In absorbing Bireley's Inc. and Gaines Food Co., General Foods probably could have used excess capacity in its extant channels of distribution and marketing activities. Certainly many retail outlets would stock General Foods' older line as well as its newly acquired citrus beverages and dog foods.

High node commonalities are every bit as strikingly apparent in several of American Home Products' acquisitions. Many economies in production, management, or marketing appear probable in some of these mergers. Similarly, many of Borden's acquisitions suggest relatively high degrees of node commonality between the acquired firms and the Borden Company. If Borden's technological and marketing bases are carefully defined, then some of the acquisitions are not nearly so unrelated as Representative Celler maintained.

In brief, then, the concept of conglomerate mergers by 1950 came to include all nonhorizontal, nonvertical mergers and embraced a sizable spectrum of node commonality.

The Interest of Economists and of Congress in Conglomerate Mergers

Concern about conglomerate mergers generally emphasized two issues: (1) the concentration of asset ownership, and (2) the competitive superiority of conglomerate firms over single-market firms. The lawmakers appeared to be concerned primarily with the first threat, the sociopolitical implications; economists' testimony indicated a greater concern with the competitive economic effects.

The amended Section 7 is interested, all in all, in merger consequences. For the Act to be effective regarding conglomerate mergers, it would seem necessary to know those consequences. But conglomerate-merger consequences are considerably more difficult to explicate than those of horizontal or vertical mergers. Unfortunately, the legislators seemed content to keep their analyses of implications at the sociopolitical level, a level to which the wording of the amended Act does not explicitly relate.[56] As we have seen, even the FTC, the most actively interested agency, failed to undertake a study of the components and consequences of conglomerate mergers.

The absence of thorough economic investigations extended, indeed, to all types of mergers. Mergers of any type lead to increased concentration of assets, and horizontal mergers lead to increased market concentration as well. In view of the apparent Congressional preoccupation with concentration, the absence of economic investigations of the implications of concentration is not readily understandable.[57]

---

[56] But see *Brown Shoe Co., Inc.* v. *U.S.*, at notes 27–28, 71–72 and accompanying text for comments on protection of competition and of competitors.

[57] Derek C. Bok, "Section 7 of the Clayton Act and the Merging of Law and Economics," *Harvard Law Review*, LXXIV (December, 1960), pp. 236–237.

Chapter IV

INDUCEMENTS FOR
CONGLOMERATE MERGERS

SCHOLARLY analyses of diversification are few. Although a body of literature on the motivations for diversifying and practical suggestions for undertaking it exists, it is for the most part descriptive rather than analytical and does not advance very much any understanding of the underlying forces making for diversification.

The central questions about diversification decisions are: (1) What general forces lead to the decision to diversify? (2) Once the general decision to diversify is made, what additional considerations give rise to the decision to undertake diversification externally (through merger) rather than internally (through investment)? (3) What is the degree of node commonality typically found in diversification; and is node commonality typically much different in instances of internal and external diversification? (4) To what degree are efficiencies possible in conglomerate firms, and what conditions suggest the greatest possibility for efficiencies to be realized?

These questions constitute the focus in this chapter.

THE MODEL OF THE FIRM

The forces that lead to diversification, and the forces that lead to a choice between internal investment and merger can best be understood in the context of firm growth. Understanding the character of these forces requires a conceptualization of the firm. At the outset we need to make an assumption about the goals of the decision makers in the firm.

For the purposes of this discussion it will suffice to assume a goal of long-run profit maximization. To be sure, a firm does many things in the short run that are not attempts at immediate maximization of profits. But short-run non-profit-maximizing behavior is consistent with this long-run goal, which finds general acceptance in the economic and business literature and would appear to be a reasonably accurate statement about most firms in the economy.[1]

Secondly, in the model, the firm is a pool of productive resources whose allocation among different uses and over time is determined by administrative decision. Thirdly, for each major functional activity in the firm there is an "optimal" (lowest-cost) level of the activity. And when all activities are functioning at optimal levels, the firm enjoys the lowest average total cost of production per unit. A constant task of the firm is the reconciliation of the various activities, attempting to move toward the "optimum firm" scale. Fourthly, a

---

[1] Clearly, the assumption as to managerial goals is critical. The crucial question would appear to be, "Does the long-run profit maximization assumption provide better explanations of behavior in single and multiproduct firms than any other assumption?"

Support for the long-run profit maximization assumption, while acknowledging the neglect of certain constraints, is provided in a critical discussion by Baldwin. In particular, Baldwin contends that "If we want a theory of managerial enterprise which assumes a single organizational objective subject to maximization or minimization, profit does appear to be more realistic than any of the alternatives offered. The advantages of such a unified theory are substantial if we want to apply theoretical analysis to markets involving a number of firms, to prediction and evaluation of industrial performance, and to problems of public policy. The findings . . . strongly suggest, although the contention is in no way definitively proven, that profit maximization is a fairly close approximation of actual motives of the typical large corporation and that any losses suffered by abstracting from the complexity of interplay among real-world motives will be *relatively minor*." (Emphasis added.) William L. Baldwin. "The Motives of Managers, Environmental Restraints, and the Theory of Managerial Enterprise," *The Quarterly Journal of Economics*, LXXVIII (May, 1964), pp. 253–254.

Any descriptive theory based on long-run profit maximizing under uncertainty, i.e., in the real world, is necessarily far less restrictive than if it were based on short-run profit maximization. Indeed, the difference between long-run profit maximization and other stated long-run goals is largely just the choice of words. For the long-run case, these goals all have to mean about the same thing.

general managerial type of excess capacity termed "organizational slack" frequently occurs in the firm. Let us look at these components of the model in greater detail.[2]

The firm may be thought of as a behavioral entity—an active participant attempting to resolve internal conflict, avoiding uncertainty, searching for productive uses for its resources and for alternative solutions when faced with a problem, and learning through experience. The material resources of the firm, as well as the experience of its personnel, are significant in the determination of the specific activities the firm undertakes. Thus, the resources of the firm determine, in large part, what the firm perceives in the external world and how the firm responds to changes in that world. For example, changes in the knowledge possessed by managerial personnel might not only change the productive services of particular resources but might also change the demand function as "seen" by the firm.

Management allocates resources among the activities of the firm in accordance with the primary goal of long-run profit maximization. The activities of the firm may be generalized to five categories, each having its own optimum scale; all have to be "reconciled" to achieve an "optimum firm." The five categories and the respective forces shaping them are: (1) the technical forces making for a technical optimal size, (2) the managerial forces making for an optimal managerial unit, (3) the financial forces making for an optimal financial unit, (4) the influences of marketing making for an optimal marketing unit, and (5) the forces of risk and fluctuation making for a unit possessing the greatest power of survival in the face of industrial vicissitudes.[3]

The web of relationship among the major functional activities in the firm is a cause of continuing allocation decisions.

---

[2] The author's indebtedness to three works is clear: E. T. Penrose, *The Theory of the Growth of the Firm* (New York: John Wiley, 1959); E. A. G. Robinson, *The Structure of Competitive Industry* (Chicago: The University of Chicago Press, 1958); and Richard M. Cyert and James G. March, *A Behavioral Theory of the Firm* (Englewood Cliffs, N. J.: Prentice-Hall, 1963).

[3] See Robinson, *op. cit.*, p. 11.

The various activities of the firm may at a given time constitute a relationship pattern in which the firm experiences the
lowest average total cost per unit of every product, but this
is unlikely. Such a pattern would be that of an optimal firm,
and there would be no tendency to depart from the scale of
operations at which it obtains. However, the uncertainty of
the real world virtually precludes a firm's achieving and
maintaining an optimal scale. Thus, management is always
adjusting the magnitude and direction of its marketing, production, managerial, finance, or risk-absorption activities in
order to attain a lower cost relationship.

The necessity to change the allocation of resources in order
to reconcile the various optima is most germane to this discussion of diversification. If, for example, production's optimum scale exceeds marketing's optimum scale, then excess
capacity will exist in the former or the marketing function
must operate at an excessive and inefficient scale. In either
case, reconciliation of the optima is required. In this situation
the reconciliation may involve, e.g., the entering of new geographic markets with current products, or the entering of
new product markets with products amenable to current production techniques, or further penetration of current product
and geographic markets by supplemental marketing branches.
We have mentioned organizational slack as being a more
generalized kind of excess capacity. Its absorption may be
due more to the entire firm's coming under competitive stress
than to any overt effort to eliminate it. Althought it is clearly
a less specific excess capacity than appears in imbalances
between optima, its presence does provide implications for
growth, diversification, and manner-of-diversification decisions.

Thus the model of the firm itself indicates that imbalances
between the various optima of the firm or the presence of
general organizational slack makes inevitable the existence of
excess capacity in one or several operations of the firm; the
absorption of this excess capacity by reconciling the optima
is a managerial activity that frequently leads to diversification.

INDUCEMENTS FOR GROWTH

What are the inducements that lead to growth in a profit-seeking firm? Most importantly, what are the implications of growth for diversification? We may now confront the former question directly, and lead toward answers to the latter.

A firm can increase profits by increasing revenues, or by decreasing costs, or by a combination of both. As for cost savings, certain economies may be achieved only in growth and diminish or disappear with the termination of growth. This circumstance suggests that there is no one absolute optimal size for a firm but that the optimum state is solely a matter of relationship among the various optima. The never-ending quest to utilize excess capacity and achieve economies may in itself induce growth. Indeed, at the limit, any idle piece of equipment, any unused technical knowledge or organizational resource possessed by the firm constitutes a production opportunity and an opportunity for savings.[4] As long as expansion can provide a way of using the firm's resources more profitably, the firm has an incentive for expanding; and as long as any resources are not used fully, there exists an incentive for finding a way of using them more completely. Unused productive capacities are essentially "free"; this alone makes it highly attractive to employ them.

Nor is it only an uncertain world that makes imbalances among the several optima the rule rather than the exception. It is also, in large part, resource rigidities that account for the existence of excess capacity. Many inputs are available only in large indivisibilities, and they do not lend themselves to immediate adjustment for day-to-day output changes. When the rate of growth is slow, indivisibilities are found not so much in the organizational aspects as in the durability of the assets, and excess capacity is the result of fluctuations

---

[4] See Eli W. Clemens, "Price Discrimination and the Multiple-Product Firm" reprinted in American Economic Association, *Readings in Industrial Organizaton and Public Policy* (Homewood, Illinois: Richard D. Irwin, 1958), pp. 263 ff.

or unexpected shifts in demand and of technological revolutions.[5] The location of the excess capacity is determined largely by the stage of development of the particular firm. For example, in the early stages of a rapidly rising firm with vigorous, capable management, the management unit may be capable of handling more work, whereas in later stages of growth excess capacity may appear in the marketing segment.

In short, at any point in time the firm is characterized by a given set of resources and input and output activities and patterns. With a goal of long-run profit maximization, management determines how best to allocate resources. Because excess capacity is virtually always present, rational management must continually ask how excess capacity can best be employed. That is, in what direction should the firm move— in greater depth in current markets and productive activities, or into new geographic markets and new product markets, or in some combination of these activities? And how would it be best to pursue this growth—through internal investment or through merger? Given the fact that in a profit-maximizing firm growth largely results from the pursuit of efficiencies, management needs to appraise opportunity costs of current growth patterns and the direction and means of alternative patterns.

DIVERSIFICATION IN THE FIRM

The stimuli leading to decisions to diversify into new markets and activities, either closely or distantly related to the existing operation, may be of several types. First, there are many external stimuli for diversification. Market saturation or lack of market growth relative to supply may lead a firm to expand in new directions. Intensified competition in one or more of the firm's markets may make expansion in those markets feasible only by expensive selling efforts and acceptance of lower profit margins. An external event, such as the

---

[5] See Joel Dean, *Managerial Economics* (Englewood Cliffs, N. J.: Prentice-Hall, 1951), pp. 115-120.

expiration of another firm's patent or access to a new technological breakthrough, may also make the opportunity costs of present markets very high. Difficulties in obtaining raw materials, experienced labor, or specialized technical or managerial personnel may constitute formidable blockages to expansion along existing lines. The risk of antitrust action may be an inducement to diversify, particularly for a large firm that already enjoys a significant share of a market. This inducement is especially important at present and will probably continue to be significant.

Secondly, some inducements arise from internal sources. Virtually all internal inducements to diversity can be visualized either as absorption of excess capacity in the major functional activities, absorption of organizational slack, or reduction of risk (risk absorption). For example, excess capacity in disposable liquid capital might best be applied to internal investment in new products or new geographic markets; or it might best be used for buying another firm in markets new to the acquiring firm. Organizational slack is a type of excess capacity whereby managers to some extent maximize personal-preference functions rather than, as in times of stress, the organization's goals. Under certain circumstances its absorption might best be accomplished through diversification. Or if current activities of the firm excessively threaten the firm's long-run viability, a reduction of risk may be undertaken. The absorption of risk is frequently effected by diversifying into counter-cyclically demanded products and new geographic markets. There are, to be sure, other internal inducements to diversify that cannot be traced to absorption of excess capacity. However, the majority and perhaps the most important inducements can be so classified.[6]

---

[6] Examination of three well-known studies of diversification motives shows that virtually all motives cited are in some form subsumed by the concept of absorption of excess capacity. See W. L. Thorp and W. F. Crowder, *The Structure of Industry*, T.N.E.C. Monograph 27 (Washington, D. C.: U.S. Government Printing Office, 1941), Part VI; Kenneth R. Andrews, "Product Diversification and the Public Interest," *Harvard Business Review*, XXIX (July, 1951); and Thomas A. Staudt, "Program for Product Diversification," *Harvard Business Review*, XXXII (November-December, 1954).

We can also identify three internal sources of information about opportunities to absorb excess capacity profitably. These are research sources, and may be broken down into the somewhat arbitrary categories of (1) market research (research on existing and new product and geographic markets, frequently effected through feedback from the marketing organization of the firm), (2) product research (research applied to products in existing or potential markets), and (3) basic research (the seeking of new ideas, not necessarily connected with any existing product or market).

Bases of Specialization and Node Commonality in Diversification

If the firm decides that its long-run profits can indeed best be maximized by diversification, what "direction" and "gap" will that diversification tend to take? That is, what typically is the general degree of node commonality in diversification and, more particularly, in diversification-through-merger as opposed to internal diversification?

The concept of *bases of specialization* will assist in answering the question. Bases of specialization are implicit in the reconciliation of optima in an uncertain world. The concept is fundamental to an understanding of rational diversification. Simply stated, in its continual adaptations to an uncertain world, the firm acquires *inter alia* a set of particular experiences, particular resources, particular operating patterns and experience, and particular good-will in market relations. It is the on-going commitment of resources to activities that results in a "character" peculiar to each firm. The exact set that is gradually acquired probably establishes a predisposition for further activities in the same general areas, unless, of course, there are strong inducements for change as discussed above.

It is too narrow, however, to think of bases of specialization merely as historical commitments and acquired expertise. Frequently a firm overtly seeks to develop a particular ability and strength in a broadly defined area and thus to achieve a special competitive position. Indeed, in the long run it may well be that the profitability, growth, and survival of a firm depend on its ability to establish one or more durable bases from which it can adapt and extend its operations. These are its bases of specialization.

We have, then, three central elements to consider in explaining the desirability (and probability) of a firm's diversifying into fields somewhat or highly related to extant operations: bases of specialization, absorption of excess capacity, and limited managerial rationality in an uncertain world. Clearly, no firm is entirely free to produce anything that happens to be in strong demand, for exploitable demand is a function of its short-run internal attributes. It would be only for products amenable to existing techniques and skills that the cross-elasticity of supply would be other than very low or zero. The limitation of exploitable demand is pertinent even for an entirely new firm with no resources other than the entrepreneurial skill and some capital, for these alone constrain choice and hence the range of exploitable opportunities.

What, then, can be said about the influence of existing resources on mode of diversification—internally through investment as opposed to merger? It appears that the influence of existing resources in shaping the direction of diversification is more important in internal than in external diversification. At the limit, the only restriction on the direction of diversification by merger is that set by entrepreneurial ability to discover appropriate firms and to negotiate and implement the acquisition. Nevertheless, in spite of this relative freedom of choice, completely unrelated diversification is rare simply because technological and marketing links with the new products give the firm a stronger competitive position.[7] Diversification with virtually no node commonality is necessarily an

---

[7] It is unusual not to find some connections in marketing, production, purchasing, research, or other activities. See the comments by George J. Stigler in "Forward" to Michael Gort, *Diversification and Integration in American Industry*, National Bureau of Economic Research (Princeton: Princeton University Press, 1962), p. xix.

act of pure investment. In a long-run profit-maximizing firm, diversification mergers of this pure-investment type would logically aim at absorbing risk—i.e., mergers into counter-cyclically demanded products to achieve earnings stability.

Pure-investment diversification is probably an extremely infrequent phenomenon. Even when merging firms operate in separate geographic markets, they frequently buy economically related products. When merging firms operate in separate product markets, they may not only buy economically related products but may have products that complement one another in a product assortment or that are imperfect substitutes for one another—in either case, the products are susceptible to joint promotion and distribution.

Gort's findings support this "relatedness" view. He argues that, choosing among activities equally attractive, a firm will usually undertake those for which the technical propinquity to its own primary activity is greatest. At least three considerations explain this disposition: (1) When the prospective new products are similar to those already produced, management is more likely to be aware of them as diversification possibilities. (2) Management's previous experience presumably gives the firm an advantage in the new activities over other entrants from other sectors of the economy. (3) When old and new products are technologically related, the existing plant, equipment, and personnel may be sufficient to produce the new ones (indeed, if so, a firm may even enter a declining industry in order to use excess capacity).[8]

Acquisition inducements

What specifically are the advantages to a long-run profit-maximizing firm in diversifying externally rather than internally?

Acquisition implies that purchase of another firm is considered a cheaper method of expansion than internal investment. There must of course be an extant firm which is willing

---

[8] *Ibid.*, p. 108.

to part with its assets at a price equal to or less than their value as seen by the potential buyer. The price must also be less than the investment outlay (including the opportunity cost of all resources) required for the expanding firm to build the necessary plant, markets, and trade connections.[9]

A number of advantages seem relatively general to entry through merger. First, that new facilities may be brought under operational control more quickly through mergers than internally. Second, that the desired facilities may be acquired more cheaply through stock purchase than replacement value of the firm's assets. Third, the services of desired personnel may be obtained outright through acquisition of the company.

The factor of risk is important for diversification and helps to explain why firms may diversify by merger. Simply stated, a new product, new organization, or new process is usually obtained with less risk by merger than by internal innovation. There are at least two main reasons for this: (1) the acquired items have already demonstrated their earning capability, and (2) they are already in an on-going situation, with goodwill, brand or enterprise recognition, and established market shares and relationships. External expansion precludes the necessity of combatting difficult competition in the early stages of development. A corollary to the preceding is that market control may be secured more rapidly and with less effort through acquisition than by internal expansion.

Acquisition also tends to impose lesser problems of financing diversification than internal growth. Sellers are frequently more willing than the investing public to accept stock. The quickly attained greater size often opens new avenues to

---

[9] An example of merger allegedly used as an entry-facilitating device is seen in the Crocker-Anglo California Bank-Citizens National Bank of Los Angeles merger. The president of the merged Crocker-Citizens National Bank stated that acquisition was "the only economic way" for Crocker-Anglo to enter the Los Angeles Area. Some of the reasons he cited for external rather than internal entry were a shortage of competent banking personnel, a drain on earnings if the expansion were undertaken internally, and the inadvisability of seeking outside capital to finance such a move. *San Francisco Chronicle*, June 15, 1965, p. 55.

additional financing. All in all, acquisition may serve as a less risky and competitively and financially more expedient form of growth. Preceding comments established that the desire to absorb excess capacity is the greatest general inducement for diversification. If merger is frequently the most advantageous form of growth, then in the presence of a merger opportunity, the desire to absorb excess capacity may be reinforced. Hence the expediency of merger may lead to more diversification in the economy than if external growth were not possible.[10]

EFFICIENCIES IN CONGLOMERATE MERGERS

The basic motive for diversifying, then, is the desire to absorb excess capacity in one form or another when that capacity cannot be used otherwise or employed as cheaply by extending current activities. Given the motivation to diversify, reasons of economy and expediency frequently impel firms to choose merger. For reasons developed earlier in this chapter, it is equally apparent that most of the resulting conglomerate mergers probably have a high degree of node commonality. It is as incorrect to say that conglomerate mergers never promote economic efficiency as it is to say that conglomerate mergers always do.[11]

Economies of size

Large firms frequently realize cost advantages simply because of their size. Some of these advantages can be attained by large conglomerate firms with high node commonality. A

---

[10] There are, of course, other inducements for mergers and specifically for diversification through merger. However, the ones cited above probably constitute the major market forces. For a substantial cross-section of merger motivations, see: J. F. Weston, *The Role of Mergers in the Growth of Large Firms* (Berkeley and Los Angeles: University of California Press, 1953), pp. 74–75 and 85–86; *Corporate Mergers and Acquisitions*, Senate Report No. 132, 85th Cong., 1st Sess. (1957) *passim*; and Myles L. Mace and George C. Montgomery, Jr., *Management Problems of Corporate Acquisitions* (Boston: Harvard University, 1962), esp. pp. 15–26.

[11] For a somewhat different point of view see John M. Blair, "The Conglomerate Merger in Economics and Law," *The Georgetown Law Journal*, XLVI (Summer, 1958), pp. 680 ff.

significant commonality of inputs clearly can enhance economies in purchasing raw material. With manufacturing or pro-
cessing commonalities, economies accrue through intrafirm
joint use of plant and equipment, and utilization of by-
products, scrap, and managerial knowledge. Savings in in-
surance and in shared administrative, research, and technical
services are often feasible. Indeed, some economies can accrue to the large conglomerate with low node commonality;
as for example, when particular supplies can be purchased
for the entire firm.

Sales promotion economies

Some economies in conglomerate firms do not depend in-
trinsically on size. Sales-promotion activities, for example,
are most prevalent if the product is differentiable by brand,
trademark, or other distinctions having potential "meaning"
in a market. While it is difficult to infer any systematic functional promotion-to-sales relationships, Bain's findings permit
an inference that conglomerate mergers of substantial size
and with a high commonality of marketing nodes are best
able to achieve sales-promotion economies.[12] But even small
operations with high commonality can benefit. The conglomerate of any size achieves substantial promotion economies if
some products of the acquiring and acquired firms (1) are
differentiable, (2) are demand complementary or can be marketed in the same product assortment; and (3) are equally
susceptible to vertical-integration in the channel of distribution or can be handled by the same independent middlemen.
If all conditions exist, economies are feasible not only in promotion but in physical handling and distribution. In short,
economies in marketing activities are largely a function of the
degree of marketing node commonality; size may increase the
advantages.

---

[12] See J. S. Bain, "Advantages of the Large Firm: Production, Distribution
and Sales Promotion," *Journal of Marketing*, XX (April, 1956), pp. 339–342.

Multiplant economies

As has been noted, some conglomerate mergers involve geo-graphically separate markets. Bain's findings on multiplant economies apply to these market-extension conglomerate mergers. To a somewhat lesser extent they are relevant also to the more common case of product-market conglomerate mergers. If economies of a certain range are found for geographically separate plants producing the same products, then multiplant economies to some extent might obtain for separate plants producing different products.

Bain believed that the rather negligible multiplant economies he found resulted from greater efficiency, in varying degrees, in central management, accounting and financial departments, legal departments, production control, labor relations, procurement, engineering, research and development, and financing costs.[13] Many of these were mentioned previously as economies which are a function of size and therefore relevant in all conglomerates, whether with separate geographic markets or separate product markets. But Bain's findings on multiplant economies were based on the same products being made at separate locations. Thus, it would be the large *market-extension* conglomerates which would be the most likely to attain whatever multiplant economies were possible—due to the commonalities of inputs and central administrative and technical services exploitable in the merged entity.

With their high commonality of management knowledge, market-extension conglomerate mergers provide full opportunity to absorb excess management capacity and to exploit economies of scale in the use of management. The situation is less clear with product-market conglomerate mergers. If a firm's diversification takes place in fields closely related to the existing activities of the firm, the management effort required

---

[13] *Ibid.*, p. 339.

per dollar of expansion is less, however, than with equal expansion into less related fields. Thus, for example, product-assortment mergers permit considerable managerial economies whereas pure-investment mergers permit virtually none.

SUMMARY

A profit-maximizing firm constantly adjusting the scope and direction of its various activities to an uncertain world acquires a particular "character"—a pattern of allocating managerial knowledge and material and financial resources to processes and markets so that "bases of specialization" develop. These bases of specialization provide the firm with special competitive positions—positions of reduced risk because of the firm's particular competence and depth in these areas.

The profit-maximizing firm is induced to grow in one direction or another because in an uncertain world adjustments to changing conditions are necessarily imperfect. Thus, there is a constant situation in the firm of excess capacity in some activity or activities. The absorption of this excess, often achieved only through growth, provides savings and results in a lower average total cost condition—and probably increased profits.

A firm may choose to emphasize lateral growth into new geographic and product markets. Diversification in one or both of these forms occurs in the contemporary economy in large part because of one or more of the following factors: (1) Intense competition and market saturation make further penetration of current markets uneconomic; hence absorption of excess management, production, finance, or marketing capacity requires movement into new markets and activities. (2) Antitrust constraints suggest, particularly to the large firm, that some existing market shares should not be increased; ventures into new product and geographic markets are undertaken as an alternative. (3) If sizable excess capacity in disposable funds exists, the firm is predisposed to diversify for pure investment or risk purposes.

With the notable exception of pure-investment diversification, firms commonly diversify into markets that are relatively highly related in management, production, or marketing aspects, chiefly because the absorption of excess capacity can best be accomplished by growth in activities with high node commonalities to extant activities. Thus, there are many implications for economies and efficient use of resources in diversification. Indeed, with a particularly high commonality of nodes between old and new activities, substantial efficiencies can be effected.

Diversification (and growth in general) through mergers rather than internally is often the more economical avenue. Not only may new facilities be operated more quickly through mergers, but the desired facilities frequently may be acquired more cheaply through stock purchase than through internal investment. The development internally of a new product or a new geographic market is often far more risky than the acquisition of an established market activity. Entry-by-merger risk is lower because the acquired items have already demonstrated their earning capability and they are currently in an on-going situation with established goodwill, brand or enterprise recognition, and supply and demand market shares and relationships. All the advantages to the profit-maximizing firm of diversifying into high-commonality activities are equally attainable by diversification through merger and diversification internally. However, merger is a more versatile means of diversification, for unlike internal investment, merger facilitates diversifying into completely unrelated activities, the so-called pure-investment diversification.

Under several conditions conglomerate mergers clearly may effect economies. Because management usually undertakes diversification to absorb capacity extant in one form or another, the typical high-node-commonality nature of either internal or external diversification implies opportunity for efficiencies. However, regardless of the degree of node commonality, some economies are possible in any merger of large firms—when cost advantages may be realized simply because of large size as, for instance, with the utilization of central administrative services. Moreover, when the merged entity is large and there is as well high node commonality in production or marketing activities, substantial efficiencies may be realized. Market extension and high-commonality product-market conglomerate mergers are cases in point. In general, the higher the node commonality the greater the economies —at the limit, equaling in magnitude those attainable in horizontal mergers.

Chapter V

SELECTED
CONGLOMERATE MERGER
CASES

THE Federal Trade Commission and the Antitrust Division of the Department of Justice have brought legal action under the amended Section 7 against a limited number of mergers designated in whole or part as "conglomerate mergers" and also against other mergers similar in alleged behavior and consequences. Both cases officially listed as conglomerate mergers and others not so listed but related through structure, alleged behavior, and alleged probable consequences, are discussed in this chapter. The central question in this discussion is essentially: "What theoretical economic inferences regarding conglomerate merger effects may be deduced from the administrative agencies' charges and approaches to the cases?" We must assume that the administrative agencies' theories are revealed in their charges and arguments. Therefore, the sources used in this analysis are primarily public transcripts of initial charges and records of Commission and court reviews and orders.[1] No value judgment is intended by concentrating almost exclusively on the arguments of the administrative agencies.

THEORIES EVIDENT IN THE CASES

The theories of economic behavior and consequences of conglomerate mergers evident in the agencies' allegations and opinions fall into three groups: (1) wealth, (2) potential competition, and (3) reciprocity.

---

[1] Sufficient citation is included to assist the interested reader in further investigation along legal lines.

Wealth

The common theme in these cases is that in each instance there is an improved ability of a corporation to deal with the rigors of the market place by the merger. Specifically, there is in each wealth case some form of subsidy of the acquired firm by the acquiring firm. The particular subsidies take the form either of purely financial aid or occur in such forms as managerial and marketing assistance.

The arguments set forth in mergers with high node commonality, such as some product assortment mergers, frequently stress the joint product and promotional economies accruing to the merged entity. Cases dealing with low-node-commonality mergers tend to stress purely financial aid. One of the latter is a merger of vertically related companies argued on the basis of the wealth theory.[2]

Potential competition

It was charged in several cases that the mergers eliminated potential competition between the acquiring and acquired firms and therefore would probably substantially lessen competition in the relevant market. Potential competition was posed in several forms. One referred to acquiring and acquired firms which had before the merger sold in separate geographic or product markets, but which had a good chance of eventual intermarket penetration. Merger made *potential* competition impossible, whereas the probable entry, given certain market conditions, of either firm into the other's product or geographic market or the entry of both into a common market would have provided salutary effects on competition.

Market-extension mergers raise the potential-competition problem. This type involves geographic diversification and occurs when a firm acquires other firms with their own local markets producing virtually the same product as the acquir-

---

[2] For reasons discussed at pp. 129–130, the arguments found in *Matter of Reynolds Metals Company*, FTC Docket 7009, are relevant to this analysis even though the merger is vertical.

ing firm. The acquired firms might have eventually constituted competition for the acquiring firm either in their markets or as entrants in the latter's markets. The first complaint
challenging a conglomerate merger of any kind was a market-
extension merger of this type.[3]

Reciprocity

The administrative agencies have argued that the persuasive power a conglomerate may exert upon suppliers who are
also potential customers may under certain circumstances
tend to lessen competition substantially.

EXAMPLES OF THE THEORIES

In some cases, the administrative agencies stated that more
than one of the foregoing issues was involved. In such instances, the case is classified here as an example of the theory
that appears to have been of primary concern.

Wealth cases

Five cases emphasized the wealth issue. One, Procter &
Gamble-Clorox, is perhaps the best known of all conglom-
erate-merger cases. It was considered by the full Federal
Trade Commission, and the final order was issued December
15, 1963. Other wealth cases are General Foods, Reynolds
Aluminum, Scott Paper, and Union Carbide.

Procter & Gamble-Clorox.—The Procter & Gamble-Clorox
case resulted in several actions.[4] Because of its precedent-set-
ting character, the case is considered here in more detail
than the other four wealth cases.

---

[3] *In the Matter of Foremost Dairies, Inc.,* FTC Docket 6495, dated January 17, 1956.

[4] The chronology of major events is as follows: (1) August 1, 1957, Procter & Gamble acquired Clorox; (2) FTC Docket 6901, complaint issued
against the merger, September 30, 1957; (3) "Initial Cease and Desist Order"
(Commerce Clearing House, Trade Regulation Reporter, paragraph 28,881),
July 11, 1960; (4) "Remand Order" (C.C.H. Trade Regulation Reporter,
paragraph 15,245), June 15, 1961; (5) "Second Initial Order to Cease and
Desist" (C.C.H. Trade Regulation Reporter, paragraph 15,773), February
28, 1962; (6) "Final Order to Cease and Desist" (C.C.H. Trade Regulation
Reporter, paragraph 16,673), December 15, 1963.

The Commission's decision, supporting many of the allegations of the FTC counsel, is based on five major factors: ·

(1) The relative disparity in size and strength between
Procter and the largest firms of the bleach industry; (2) the
excessive concentration in the industry at the time of the
merger, and Clorox's dominant position in the industry; (3)
the elimination, brought about by the merger, of Procter as a
potential competitor of Clorox; (4) the position of Procter in
other markets; and (5) the nature of the "economies" enabled
by the merger.[5]

Procter & Gamble, the nation's largest manufacturer of
packaged detergents and household cleaning agents, in purchasing Clorox effected a product-extension merger. The
products of both firms were used complementarily and were
closely associated in the minds of consumers. Both firms'
products were also closely related in the manner in which
they were marketed: both being low-cost, high-turnover consumer goods, they were sold through the same channels, and
both were presold through mass advertising and sales promotion.[6] The testimony of one Procter executive regarding the
close relationship of managerial and promotional experience
between the acquiring and acquired firms supported these
characterizations:

> While this is a completely new business for us, taking us for
> the first time into the marketing of a household bleach and
> disinfectant, we are thoroughly at home in the field of manu-
> facturing and marketing low-priced, rapid turn-over con-
> sumer products.[7]

Before the acquisition Clorox had advertised extensively
but had not engaged in sales promotions such as two-for-one
offers, premiums, and similar programs typically undertaken
by Procter. In 1957 Clorox spent $1,750,000 for newspaper ad-
vertising, $560,000 for magazine advertising, $258,000 for

---

[5] "Final Order to Cease and Desist," *op. cit.*, p. 21,558.
[6] *Ibid.*
[7] *Ibid.*, p. 21,566.

radio and billboard advertising, and $1,150,000 for television advertising. Advertising expenditures were approximately 10 percent of total sales.[8]

Clorox had approximately 50 percent of the national sales of liquid bleach. Purex, the second-largest firm, had about 15 percent of the national market. Two other firms accounted for another 10 percent of the sales, making approximately 75 percent of the national sales controlled by four firms. Clorox, however, was the only firm selling nationally; Purex competed in only part of the country.

Purex manufactured a number of products including an abrasive cleanser, a toilet soap, and detergents. Total sales of all its products were approximately $50 million in 1957. Clorox limited itself primarily to the production and sale of liquid bleach; its sales in 1957 were approximately $40 million, and its assets $12.6 million. Procter had total 1957 sales of approximately $1,156 million and 1958 assets of $756 million.

The Commission dealt with the structure of the acquired firm's market at some length:

> Economists teach and Congress postulated, that market behavior follows market structure; hence, proof that a merger has created or aggravated a market structure conducive (in a practical, not theoretical or abstract sense) to practices that substantially lessen competition, or tend to monopoly, is sufficient under the statute.[9]

As to the impact of the merger on conditions of entry, the Commission said:

> Procter, by increasing the Clorox advertising budget, by engaging in sales promotions far beyond the capacity of Clorox's rivals, and by obtaining for Clorox the advertising savings to which Procter, as a large national advertiser, is entitled, is in a position to entrench still further the already settled consumer preference for the Clorox brand, and thereby make

[8] *Ibid.*, p. 21,563.
[9] *Ibid.*, p. 21,573.

entry even more forbidding than it was prior to the merger. In addition, because a multiproduct firm of large size enjoys . . . very substantial competitive advantages in an industry marked by product differentiation through mass advertising, sales promotion, shelf display and related merchandising methods, the prospects become increasingly remote, given the substitution of Procter for Clorox in the liquid bleach industry, that small or medium-sized firms will be minded to enter the industry. The scale of optimally efficient operation in the industry has been so increased, by reason of Procter's advertising that only very large firms—firms on the scale of Procter itself—can reasonably be expected to be able to compete on roughly equal terms in the industry.[10]

The Commission said that finding a structural change to constitute a lessening of the market's competitive character did not depend on Procter's conduct after the merger. It held that it was not necessary to ascertain or predict whether and to what extent Procter had taken or would take action to effect for Clorox the potential advantages, such as those of scale, accruing from the merger.[11] Size was relevant, the Commission said; but primarily "disparity of size, not absolute size, has importance in a merger case of this kind."[12] It elaborated, however, that it did not intend to suggest that size disparity is relevant in every conglomerate merger case.

The Commission conducted no analysis of Procter's position in its other markets, stating that such an analysis was undesirable if Section 7 proceedings were to be kept within reasonable bounds of simplicity. Nevertheless, the Commission

---

[10] *Ibid.*, p. 21,579. Counsel for the Commission had previously introduced evidence before the hearing examiner that for the twelve-month period ending June 30, 1958, the joint purchase of advertising by Procter & Gamble and Clorox, bought at volume discount rates, saved Clorox $138,500. The promotional and advertising support Procter gave Clorox was great, exemplified by the fact that the former spent in excess of $79 million for advertising during the fiscal year ending June 30, 1957. See also *Procter & Gamble Co.*, Docket No. 6901 (1960 Trade Regulation Reporter, paragraph 28,881), p. 37,422, and Richard C. Clark, "Conglomerate Mergers and Section 7 of the Clayton Act," *Notre Dame Lawyer*, XXXVI (May, 1961), p. 263.

[11] *Ibid.*, p. 21,579.

[12] *Ibid.*, p. 21,582.

thought it possible to infer some degree of monopoly power in Procter's other markets. It held that, at the least, Procter's manifest strength in its other markets rebuts any inference that the firm cannot enjoy the advantages that flow both from its own financial size and strength as well as those that flow from the dominant position of Clorox in its market.[13]

According to the Commission, it is the impact on Clorox's rivals and prospective-entry firms that offers the appropriate standpoint for appraising the effects of the merger. Of greatest import in this respect is the fact that Procter possesses the *potential* to conduct aggressive market tactics. Consistent with its view that conduct is determined by structure, the Commission noted that many of the conditions which shape the nature of competition in an industry are to an important degree psychological, stemming from the competitors' and potential competitors' appraisals of the intentions of others rather than from the intentions, or actions taken, themselves.[14]

The examiner's hearings were held under the aegis of the Commission's decision in Pillsbury Mills, Inc.[15] Extensive inquiry had been thought necessary in Pillsbury, but subsequent Section 7 litigation and confirmation by the Supreme Court have discouraged the assumption that broad inquiry is necessarily productive of more rational decisions.[16] When Section 7 law was even more fluid and unsettled, broad principles of materiality and relevancy may have been warranted, "but it is now clear that the path toward just and effective enforcement of the statute lies in the direction of narrowing the scope of necessary or permissible inquiry."[17]

The FTC order, which embodies many arguments raised

---

[13] *Ibid.*, p. 21,584.
[14] *Ibid.*, p. 21,559.
[15] (Docket 6000, 1960 Trade Regulation Reporter, Paragraph 29,277).
[16] "There is no reason to protract already complex antitrust litigation by detailed analyses of peripheral economic facts, if the basic issues of the case may be determined through study of a fair sample." *Brown Shoe Co.* v. *U.S.* 370 U.S. 294, 341. Also see *U.S.* v. *Philadelphia National Bank* (C.C.H. 1963 Trade Cases, paragraph 70,812), pp. 78,267–68.
[17] *Procter & Gamble*, p. 21,586.

by the Commission's counsel, relies in large part upon deductions from price theory. For example, the Commission explicitly mentions market structure as a primary determinant of market conduct (and inferentially of market performance). As a result, the Commission focused attention upon the implications of a structural change in the acquired's market, the change in period t_1 being the substitution of Procter for Clorox. It held that the latter's competitors were constrained by Procter's potential to conduct aggressive market tactics. By this argument the Commission stressed the psychological state of the current and potential competitors.

Procter & Gamble-Clorox is a merger with high node commonality, a product assortment merger in which subsidizations include not only purely financial shifting but resource shifting in forms such as joint promotional programs. The opportunity for sizable economies is high, for the high node commonality permits absorption of excess capacity in several of the common activities, especially marketing.

General Foods.—On December 31, 1957, General Foods Corporation acquired The S.O.S. Company of Chicago, the country's dominant producer and marketer of household steel wool, accounting for 51 percent of sales in the United States that year. There were only four other manufacturers of household steel wool. The second-largest company accounted for 47.6 percent of the market, with the remaining three firms splitting the balance of approximately 1.4 percent. Neither of the two largest firms had sales in excess of $17 million. General Foods' sales, by contrast, exceeded $1 billion.

The FTC complaint of September 30, 1963,[18] alleged that the acquisition might substantially lessen competition or tend to create a monopoly in the manufacture, distribution, and sale of household steel wool throughout the United States.

---

[18] *General Foods Corporation,* FTC Docket 8600 (C.C.H. Trade Regulation Reporter, paragraph 16,612), issued September 30, 1963. Order denying motion for identification of materials to be officially noticed and denying request for oral argument thereon (Trade Regulation Reporter, paragraph 16,842), issued April 3, 1964.

The Commission asserted that other current and potential producers of household steel wool had been or might be precluded from competing with General Foods because of one or more of the following factors: General Foods' dominant market position, financial resources and economic power; its advertising ability and experience; its merchandising and promotional ability and experience; its comprehensive line of packaged grocery products; its ability to command consumer acceptance of its products and of valuable grocery-store shelf space; and its ability to concentrate on one of its products or on one section of the country the full impact of its promotional, advertising, and merchandising experience and ability.

The Commission alleged that the ability of General Foods to presell its products facilitated its efforts to acquire shelf space. General Foods in 1962 was the nation's third-largest advertiser (having risen from sixth rank in 1956), spending approximately $105 million and using all media to promote its products. It received substantial advertising discounts through its volume advertising.

There is a close similarity of node commonality between the General Foods-S.O.S. merger and Procter & Gamble-Clorox. There is also a parallel in the kinds of arguments raised by the FTC counsel, stemming primarily from the acquired firm's market structure in relation to the competitive abilities of the acquiring firm.

Reynolds Metals Company.—On August 31, 1956, Reynolds Metals Company acquired Arrow Brands, Inc., Long Beach, California.[19] Arrow, a florist-foil converter, competed with about seven other companies. Arrow was the largest producer, having about 33 percent of the industry's sales. Arrow's total sales of foil products in 1955 were $497,000; Reynolds'

---

[19] *Reynolds Metal Company*, FTC Docket 7009, issued December 27, 1957. Initial order to cease and desist (Trade Regulation Reporter, paragraph 27,857), released March 20, 1959. Order to cease and desist (Trade Regulation Reporter, paragraph 28,533), issued January 21, 1960. Commission's order affirmed, *Reynolds Metal Co.* v. *Federal Trade Commission* (1962 Trade Cases, paragraph 70,471), December 27, 1962.

net sales in 1957 approximated $446,579,000.[20] The acquisition of Arrow by Reynolds, an aluminum-foil producer, was a forward, vertical merger.[21]

The Commission limited consideration to competitive effects in the level of distribution in which Arrow competed. Before the acquisition the firms at that level were keen price competitors. After acquisition, the balance of power shifted to Arrow.[22] During 1957, prices in the industry were reduced. Arrow lowered its florist-foil prices across the board, pricing some at or below cost of production. Arrow maintained the low prices from October, 1957, to the middle of 1958.

Competitors testified that Arrow's price was below their ability to meet it. The Commission asserted that Arrow could not have maintained the low prices for so long a time strictly on its own.

> In addition, it is extremely unlikely that Arrow on its own could have built a new plant valued at $500,000 or more, which it was able to do after the merger with financing from the respondent. That it could do these things after the acquisition illustrates something that is the real core of this case—Arrow . . . became, as a result of the merger, a dominating factor in this small but important industry.[23]

The District of Columbia Circuit Court of Appeals in upholding the Commission's decision said:

> The converter's assimilation into the producer's enormous capital structure and resources gave the converter an immediate advantage over its competitors. The power of the "deep pocket" or "rich parent" for one converter in an industry where previously no company was very large and all were relatively small opened the possibility and power to sell at prices approximating cost or below, thereby enabling it to undercut and ravage the less affluent competition.[24]

---

[20] 1960 Trade Regulation Reporter, paragraph 28,533, p. 37,252.
[21] *Ibid.*, p. 37,255.
[22] *Ibid.*
[23] *Ibid.*
[24] *Reynolds Metals Co.* v. *Federal Trade Commission,* (1962 Trade Cases, paragraph 70,471), p. 76,922.

But the court did not or could not, it said, intimate that the mere intrusion of bigness into a competitive economic community otherwise populated by small firms *per se* invoked the Clayton Act.[25]

The Reynolds-Arrow business relationship was a vertical one involving supplier and customer, but the court declined to base its findings of illegality on foreclosure concepts of vertical integration. The court found that evidence would not support a foreclosure of a substantial market by Reynolds in relation to the competition; moreover, the possibility that Arrow's competitors might be foreclosed from a source of supply was not mentioned. The court dealt with the case as a conglomerate merger.[26] Implications of financial shifting were a major point in the Commission's arguments. "Indeed, one might infer from the means employed by the Federal Trade Commission to invalidate the Arrow-Reynolds merger that it had set out deliberately to develop a test broad enough to comprehend a conglomerate."[27]

Scott Paper.—The Scott Paper Company, a manufacturer and marketer of sanitary paper products and household waxed paper, acquired three firms between 1951 and 1954: Soundview Pulp Co. (Everett, Washington), November 9, 1951; Detroit Sulphite Pulp and Paper Co. (Detroit), September 2, 1954; and Hollingsworth and Whitney Co. (Boston), October 27, 1954.[28] In terms of finished products, the acquired companies were not competing with Scott.[29]

---

[25] *Ibid.*, p. 76,928.

[26] "Conglomerate Mergers Under Section 7 of the Clayton Act," *The Yale Law Journal*, LXXII (May 1963), p. 1267.

[27] "The Consolidated Foods Case: A New Section 7 Test for the Conglomerate Merger," *Virginia Law Review*, XLIX (May 1963), p. 857.

[28] *Scott Paper Company*, FTC Docket 6559, issued June 1, 1956. Initial order of divestiture, July 14, 1958. Case remanded to examiner January 5, 1959. Interlocutory appeal granted October 22, 1959. Divestiture by initial order, February 1, 1960. Final order of divestiture (Trade Regulation Reporter, paragraph 29,278), issued December 16, 1960. Remanded for more information on market shares, *Scott Paper Co.* v. *Federal Trade Commission* (1962 Trade Cases, paragraph 70,271) 3rd. Cir., March 27, 1962. FTC Opinion (Trade Regulation Reporter, paragraph 16,706), issued December 26, 1963. Modified cease and desist order, May 8, 1964.

[29] Trade Regulation Reporter, paragraph 29,278, p. 37,632.

The market in which the proscribed effects allegedly would occur was Scott's market of sanitary paper products and household waxed paper. Scott was the dominant producer in the relatively concentrated market in these lines. In 1955, four firms had 66 percent of the market.[30]

According to the Federal Trade Commission Scott's acquisition of the vertically integrated Hollingsworth and Whitney was essentially a conglomerate merger, for the extensive line of paper products of the latter did not overlap Scott's. After the acquisition, Scott installed new buildings, paper machines, converting equipment, and improvements to machines at two of Hollingsworth's plants.

The Commission charged that the acquired facilities could be converted to the manufacture of Scott's products and would thereby enhance Scott's dominance.[31] The acquired facilities afforded substantial economies and marketing advantages which Scott could realize in profits or invest in increased advertising and promotional activities or further product diversification.[32]

Union Carbide.—Union Carbide Corporation of New York City acquired the Visking Corporation of Chicago on December 31, 1956.[33] Among other products, Visking manufactured synthetic sausage casings, its chief product, accounting for approximately $25.6 million in sales in 1956. Carbide did not compete for the sale of the casings; nor did it supply the materials from which the casings were made. The Commission

---

[30] *Ibid.*, pp. 37,637–37,638.

[31] See Betty Bock, *Mergers and Markets, A Guide to Economic Analysis of Law*, Studies in Business Economics 77 (New York: National Industrial Conference Board, 1962), pp. 132, 152.

[32] Trade Regulation Reporter, paragraph 29,278, p. 37,633. See also Ronald W. Donnem, "The Conglomerate Merger and Reciprocity," *The Antitrust Bulletin* (March-April 1963), p. 285, and "Scott Paper Company Gets F.T.C. Ruling to Retain Three Acquired Firms Ordered Divested," *The Wall Street Journal* (April 24, 1964), p. 10.

[33] *Union Carbide Corporation*, FTC Docket 6826, July 8, 1957. Order to cease and desist in part (Trade Regulation Reporter, paragraph 15,503), issued September 25, 1961. Divestiture order settlement (Trade Regulation Reporter, paragraph 16,638), released November 1, 1963.

described this portion of the merger as "purely conglomerate."[34]

As the leading seller of cellulose sausage casings, Visking made about 60 percent of the total national sales of the product. Visking's patents had expired, which opened the field to new entrants.[35]

The FTC contended that the acquisiton of Visking, reinforcing its assets of 38 million dollars with Carbide's 1.5 billion dollars of assets, would probably tend substantially to lessen competition in the synthetic sausage market because of the increased competitive possibilities of the conglomerate's vast wealth.

Potential competition cases

The leading examples of the potential competition issue in terms of geographic diversification are four dairy cases. The other potential competition cases in this section involve product diversification.

Dairy cases.—Foremost Dairies, Inc.[36] acquired all or part of the stock or assets of 41 dairy-products corporations in 1951–1955. During 1951–1956, Beatrice Foods Company[37] acquired all or part of the stock or assets of 44 dairy-products corporations and all or part of the assets of 87 other dairy-products concerns. During the same period, the Borden Co.[38]

---

[34] *Union Carbide Corporation*, Docket 6826 (C.C.H. Trade Regulation Reporter, paragraph 15,503), pp. 20,367–20,374.

[35] *Ibid.*, p. 20,374.

[36] *Foremost Dairies, Inc.*, FTC Docket 6495, issued January 17, 1956. Appeal of counsel in support of complaint sustained and ruling of hearing examiner reversed, June 4, 1956. Order on appeal from hearing examiner's ruling quashing subpoena, March 13, 1957. Order ruling in interlocutory appeal, February 11, 1959. Order to cease and desist (Trade Regulation Reporter, paragraph 15,877), issued April 30, 1962.

[37] *Beatrice Foods Co.*, FTC Docket 6653, issued October 16, 1956. Order denying interlocutory appeal from ruling denying motion to quash or limit subpoena duces tecum. FTC order reversed and remanded (1960 Trade Cases, paragraph 69,685), April 4, 1960. Initial order to cease and desist (Trade Regulation Reporter, paragraph 16, 831), issued March 2, 1964.

[38] *The Borden Co.*, FTC Docket 6652, issued October 16, 1956. Interlocutory appeal from ruling denying motion to quash or limit subpoena duces

acquired all or part of the stock or assets of 33 dairy-products corporations and 47 other dairy-products concerns, and National Dairy Products Corporation[39] acquired all or part of the stock or assets of 21 dairy-products corporations, one vegetable-oil manufacturer, and 18 other dairy-products concerns.[40] In Foremost Dairies, some mergers were horizontal and others involved market extension. Only the Commission's opinion as it relates to the market-extension mergers is immediately pertinent here.

According to the Commission, potential dangers to competition are created when a large conglomerate acquires a small independent firm because the merger places the remaining small firms at a serious competitive disadvantage. Their survival depends on how well they do in selling a particular product in one or a few markets, whereas the conglomerate firm's profitability and survival are determined by its market position in many products and many markets. The opinion of the Commission, written by Commissioner Dixon, holds that "the resultant disparity in size and type of operations permits the large conglomerate to strike down its smaller rivals with relatively little effort or loss in over-all profit."[41] This potential market advantage is similarly realized by a firm selling a single product in many separate markets, for

---

tecum denied March 23, 1959. Petition to require production of documents denied (1959 Trade Cases, paragraph 69,404), July 13, 1959. Petition for rehearing denied (1959 Trade Cases, paragraph 69,437), July 30, 1959. Consent to cease and desist (Trade Regulation Reporter, paragraph 16,869), issued April 15, 1964.

[39] *National Dairy Products Corp.*, FTC Docket 6651, October 16, 1956. Order denying interlocutory appeal from ruling denying motion to quash or limit subpoena duces tecum. Consent to cease and desist (Trade Regulation Reporter, paragraph 16,282), issued January 30, 1963.

[40] See Charles F. Phillips, Jr., and George R. Hall, "Economic and Legal Aspects of Merger Litigation, 1951–1962," *University of Houston Business Review*, X (Fall, 1963), pp. 85–86. See also *Mergers and Superconcentration*, Staff Report of the Select Committee on Small Business, House of Representatives, 87th Cong., November 8, 1962, pp. 26–27; and Bock, *op. cit.*, pp. 130–131.

[41] *Foremost Dairies, Inc.*, Order to cease and desist (C.C.H. Trade Regulation Reporter, paragraph 15,877), p. 20,686.

its operations in any one market are not governed solely by that market's conditions. For these reasons market-extension mergers may be viewed and judged on the same grounds as conglomerate mergers.[42]

When established firms enter new markets by acquiring the leading independent firms, they destroy potential competition in two ways: they eliminate the acquired company as a competitor in its own markets and as a potential entrant in the acquiring firm's markets. Hence these mergers dry up the most promising source of potential competition. With high market concentration, the main and frequently only restraint on market power by oligopolists is potential competition.[43]

Two arguments constituted the major thrust of the Commission's decision in Foremost Dairies. First, the market-extension mergers frequently eliminated potential competition and thus in some circumstances were believed to have the proscribed effect on competition. Secondly, because they were mergers of noncompeting products, some aspects of the wealth issue were implied. However, the primary argument in these market-extension mergers appeared to be directed toward the implications of eliminating potential competition rather than implications of the shifting of resources among the firm's markets.

El Paso Natural Gas.—Pacific Northwest Pipeline Corporation was acquired by the El Paso Natural Gas Company.[44] The issue was whether the acquisition substantially lessened competition in the sale of natural gas in California, a market in which El Paso was the sole out-of-state supplier, account-

---

[42] *Ibid.*

[43] *Ibid.*, p. 20,689. For similar arguments in two other dairy cases see *National Dairy Products* (C.C.H. 1961–1963 Trade Regulation Reporter, paragraph 16,282); "Beatrice Foods Company—Initial Decision," FTC *News Summary* (March 27, 1964), and Trade Regulation Reporter, paragraph 16,831, for text in full.

[44] Supreme Court reversed 1962 Trade Cases, paragraph 70,571, and ordered divestiture without delay. *United States* v. *El Paso Natural Gas Company, et al.* (1964 Trade Cases, paragraph 71,073), April 6, 1964.

ing for more than 50 percent of all gas consumed in California
in 1956.[45]

The effect on competition in a particular market through
acquisition of another company is determined by the nature
or extent of that market and by the nearness of the absorbed
company to it, that company's eagerness to enter that market,
its resourcefulness, and so on. Pacific Northwest's position as
a competitive factor in California was not disproved by the
fact that it had never sold gas there. Unsuccessful bidders are
no less competitors than the successful one. The presence of
two or more suppliers gives buyers a choice. Pacific Northwest
was no feeble, failing company; nor was it inexperienced and
lacking in resourcefulness. . . . It had adequate reserves and
managerial skill. It was so strong and militant that it was
viewed with concern, and coveted, by El Paso.[46]

Procter & Gamble.—As we have seen, the Procter & Gamble-Clorox competitive effects were argued primarily on the
basis of the wealth theory. However, the Commission also
alleged that the proscribed effects would in part be brought
about by the elimination of Procter as a potential competitor
of Clorox.[47]

Ekco Products Company.—The Ekco Products Company
of Chicago in 1954 acquired the McClintock Manufacturing
Company of Los Angeles, and in 1958 some assets of Black-
man Stamping and Manufacturing Company, also of Los
Angeles.[48] Ekco is a large, diversified company specializing
in the production and sale of various types of cooking ware
and commercial food-handling equipment (1959 net sales of
$73 million). McClintock was the leading producer of com-

---

[45] *U.S. v. El Paso Natural Gas Co., et al.* (C.C.H. 1964 Trade Cases,
paragraph 71,073), p. 79,232.

[46] *Ibid.,* p. 79,235.

[47] *Procter & Gamble Co.,* "Final Order to Cease and Desist" (C.C.H.
1963 Trade Regulation Reporter, paragraph 16,673), p. 21,558.

[48] *Ekco Products Co.,* FTC Docket 8122, September 26, 1960. Order as to
official notice of a legislative report, December 7, 1962. Initial order dismiss-
ing charges (Trade Regulation Reporter, paragraph 16,484), issued June 28,
1963. Order to cease and desist (Trade Regulation Reporter, paragraph
16,879), issued April 21, 1964.

mercial meat-handling equipment in the country, accounting for about 98 percent of the national sales of such equipment. (1953 total sales were approximately $1.5 million.) Blackman at the time of its acquisition was the only other company in the country selling a full line of commercial meat-handling equipment. Ekco had never manufactured or sold commercial meat-handling equipment before acquiring McClintock.

The merger allegedly tended substantially to lessen competition by (a) eliminating actual and potential competition between Ekco and the acquired companies; (b) eliminating substantial competitive entities; (c) expanding the effect in this limited market of Ekco's strength; (d) creating Ekco as the only full-line company in the market; and (e) deterring new entrants.[49]

Penn-Olin Chemical Company.—The Penn-Olin Chemical Company was formed as a joint venture of Pennsalt Chemicals and Olin Mathieson Chemical Company.[50] The joint venture was incorporated on February 25, 1960. In 1960 Pennsalt had sales of more than $90 million and assets of approximately the same amount, and Olin had sales of $690 million and assets of $860 million.[51]

Pennsalt is a 110-year-old chemical company engaged in the production and sale of about 400 chemicals and chemical products. Olin is a diversified industrial corporation. Its chemical division is one of seven and accounts for approximately 30 percent of the corporation's operating revenues. Pennsalt and Olin were not competitors and were not vertically related in regard to sodium chlorate, the line of the joint venture.[52]

[49] *Ekco Products Company*, Docket 8122 (C.C.H. Trade Regulation Reporter, paragraph 16,484). Also see "Ekco Products Company—Initial Decision," FTC *News Summary* (July 19, 1963), and FTC *News Summary* (May 15, 1964).

[50] Department of Justice complaint 1583 filed January 6, 1961. Complaint dismissed (D.C. Del. 1963) (1963 Trade Cases, paragraph 70,762), May 1, 1963. U.S. Supreme Court 1964, vacating and remanding D.C. Del., *United States v. Penn-Olin Chemical Company, et al.* (1964 Trade Cases, paragraph 71,147), June 22, 1964.

[51] *U.S. v. Penn-Olin Chemical Co., et al.* (C.C.H. 1963 Trade Cases, paragraph 70,762), p. 78,064.

[52] *Ibid.*, p. 78,073.

Pennsalt and two other companies constituted the sodium chlorate industry in the U.S. Pennsalt had experience in the manufacture and sale of sodium chlorate in the Far West and Olin had contacts with prospective customers in the Southeast. The Penn-Olin joint venture was designed to enable the two companies to strengthen their share of the Southeast market dominated by Hooker Chemical Corporation and American Potash and Chemical Corporation. In that market in 1960 Hooker supplied 46.5 percent and American Potash 41.6 percent of the sodium chlorate. Pennsalt's share, independent of the amount sold by Olin as its sale agent, was 2.1 percent; including Olin's sales it was 8.9 percent.[53]

The position of the government was that Pennsalt and Olin *could* have competed with each other since each was as financially able and otherwise competent to compete on an individual basis as other sodium chlorate manufacturers.[54]

Lever Brothers.—On May 22, 1957, Lever Brothers Company purchased the trademark for the detergent "All,"[55] and the patents relating to "All" were assigned to Lever by the selling firm, Monsanto Chemical Company.[56]

During 1954–1956, Monsanto had experienced keen competition from the other two major producers of low-sudsing, heavy-duty detergents: Procter & Gamble and Colgate. From a position in 1953 of virtually 100 percent of the low-sudsing market, "All" dropped to a market share of 55.3 percent in 1956. Monsanto found it could realize profits in the production of the raw material, but not so in the manufacture, sale, and distribution of the finished product. In 1956, Monsanto sold the marketing rights of "All" to Lever.[57]

Lever Brothers had not been successful in introducing any

---

[53] *Ibid.*

[54] *Ibid.*, p. 78,072.

[55] Department of Justice complaint 1406 filed July 8, 1958. Complaint dismissed (S.D.N.Y.) *United States* v. *Lever Brothers Company and Monsanto Chemical Company* (1963 Trade Cases, paragraph 70, 770), April 30, 1963.

[56] 1963 Trade Cases, paragraph 70,770, p. 78,099.

[57] *Ibid.*, pp. 78,104–78,105.

low-sudsing heavy detergents. At the time of its purchase of "All" it had no similar product on the market. But Lever had the experience, expertise, and organization to advertise, promote, and sell a detergent product—all of which Monsanto lacked.[58]

The government contended that the acquisition would substantially lessen competition in what it considered to be the relevant market, namely, the entire heavy-duty detergent market, for it claimed that the heavy-duty detergent market was largely concentrated in three firms: Procter, Colgate, and Lever. Therefore, the government claimed, Monsanto's sale to Lever eliminated the former as the only significant new entrant to have gained national distribution in heavy-duty detergents.

The court, however, rejected government claims that the relevant product market was heavy detergents. As in Brown Shoe,[59] it selected a narrower submarket, low-sudsing heavy-duty detergents, in which the product was separately marketed, separately advertised, and used for a distinctive purpose.

General Motors.—In 1953 General Motors Corporation acquired the Euclid Road Machinery Company.[60] General Motors was the largest manufacturing corporation in the United States. Euclid at the time of the acquisition was a leading manufacturer of off-highway earth-moving equipment and was first in the United States in production of off-highway dump trucks, accounting for approximately half of these trucks in the country.[61] Although General Motors did not manufacture off-highway earth-moving equipment before the acquisition, it did manufacture major components

[58] *Ibid.*, pp. 78,105–78,106.
[59] *U.S. v. Brown Shoe* (370 U.S. 294, 321–322). In Brown Shoe the Supreme Court held that mergers were to be functionally viewed in the context of the particular industry involved.
[60] Department of Justice complaint 1483 filed October 16, 1959. Transfer of antimerger action to another district (1960 Trade Cases, paragraph 69,665), March 25, 1960. Pending.
[61] Bock, *op. cit.*, pp. 188–189, and p. 152.

of that equipment, such as diesel engines and transmissions. Euclid in 1953 purchased more than half of its requirements for diesel engines and transmissions from suppliers other than General Motors.[62]

Before 1953 General Motors had considered entering the earth-moving equipment field through internal expansion. It had expended considerable funds in research, design, and engineering work along this line. But it acquired Euclid instead of following through on this development.

The government contended the acquisition violated Section 7 because (1) it eliminated potential competition between General Motors and Euclid in the off-highway earth-moving equipment line and (2) its reasonably probable effect would be substantially to lessen competition (a) in that line (because of General Motors' competitive advantage over other producers by reason of its integration and financial power, and because this merger might foster others in the field), (b) in the manufacture and sale of components, and (c) in the business of financing dealers' purchases and sales.[63] (Yellow Manufacturing Acceptance Corporation, a wholly-owned subsidiary of General Motors, is engaged in the latter activity.)

International Paper.—On November 6, 1956, International Paper acquired Long-Bell Lumber Corporation and Long-Bell Lumber Company.[64] The former is a holding company, the latter a leading producer of lumber in the Pacific Northwest. Long-Bell Corporation held a 12 percent stock interest in the Longview Fibre Company.

International Paper proposed to construct a kraft mill in Oregon, its first facility in the West utilizing the timber re-

---

[62] *U.S.* v. *General Motors* (C.C.H. 1960 Trade Cases, paragraph 69,665), p. 76,633, and *Corporate Mergers and Acquisitions*, Senate Report No. 132, 85th Cong., 1st Sess. (1956), p. 46.

[63] *U.S.* v. *General Motors*, as in n. 62.

[64] *International Paper Co.* FTC Docket 6676, issued November 6, 1956. Petition for injunctive relief dismissed (1957 Trade Cases, paragraph 68,-610), December 14, 1956. Consent order to cease and desist (1957-1958 Trade Regulation Reporter, paragraph 26,560), released July 3, 1957. Order consenting to transfer of stock, March 23, 1960.

sources of Long-Bell. Before the acquisition, Long-Bell had also planned to build a kraft pulp and paper plant in the area. Long-Bell's plans were dropped after the merger. The complaint held that Longview Fibre's competition would be eliminated if it were retained in the acquisition, but, if International were required to divest itself of Longview, then when International entered the market Longview would be a major competitor.[65]

Reciprocity cases

Consolidated Foods.—On April 30, 1951, Consolidated Foods Corporation of Chicago acquired Gentry, Inc. of Los Angeles.[66] The merging companies were not competitors, and sales by Gentry to Consolidated were "insubstantial."[67] Consolidated Foods was a large diversified processor and seller of food products, Gentry a manufacturer of dehydrated onion and garlic food seasonings.

Gentry was one of two dominant firms in a four-firm industry. Firms that both supplied Consolidated and bought in volume from Gentry purchased more than 25 percent of the onion produced by the industry and not quite 25 percent of the garlic.[68]

The issue was whether the merger created a serious danger that the Gentry division would acquire a protected market in which competitive opportunities would be denied other sellers of dehydrated onion and garlic through Consolidated's reciprocal buying power. Consolidated allegedly had the opportunity through the acquisition to realize a profit from sales

---

[65] *International Paper Company,* Docket 6676 (C.C.H. 1957–1958 Trade Regulation Reporter, paragraph 25,560), p. 36,252. See also *Corporate Mergers and Acquisitions,* pp. 45–46.

[66] *Consolidated Foods Corp.* FTC Docket 7000 issued December 18, 1957. Interlocutory appeal denied, March 4, 1960. FTC decision (Trade Regulation Reporter, paragraph 16,182), issued November 15, 1962. Final order to cease and desist, March 22, 1963. Reversed (CA–7 1964) (1964 Trade Cases, paragraph 71,054), March 24, 1964. Court of Appeals' ruling reversed by U.S. Supreme Court (C.C.H. Trade Regulation Reporter, paragraph 71,432), April 28, 1965.

[67] 1963 Trade Regulation Reporter, paragraph 16,182, p. 20,973.

[68] *Ibid.,* p. 20,980.

in one product area, dehydrated onion and garlic, on the
sheer strength of its buying power in other markets and not
on the basis of a better product or lower price.[69] The Commission contended that it is the relative size and conglomeration of business rivals, rather than economic efficiency, that
may determine firm growth and success, and, ultimately, the
allocation of resources.[70]

> To the extent that a diversification or congomlerate merger
> produces an industry structure that facilitates and furthers
> reciprocal buying, it is likely to lead to the most serious of
> anticompetitive consequences, viz., to confer upon the large,
> diversified corporations a crushing weapon against small,
> single-line competitors.[71]

General Dynamics Corporation.—General Dynamics Corporation acquired the Liquid Carbonic Corporation on September 30, 1957.[72] The Department of Justice asked the court
to order General Dynamics to cease requiring its suppliers to
buy carbon dioxide and other industrial gases from it and to
divest itself of its carbon-dioxide divisions.[73]

In 1961, General Dynamics was the largest defense con-
tractor in the nation, having more than $1,900 million in
defense sales for the year ended June 30, 1961. General Dynamics' over-all sales in 1961 totaled approximately $2,062
million. Liquid Carbonic Division is the largest manufacturer
and distributor of carbon dioxide in the country. In 1959, it
accounted for approximately 29 percent of the total industry
shipments of carbon dioxide, with sales value approximately
$21 million. Through twelve operating divisions, General Dy-
namics engages in the manufacture and sale of a wide variety

---

[69] *Ibid.*, pp. 20,973, 20,977.

[70] *Ibid.*, p. 20,977.

[71] *Ibid.*, p. 20,978. See also "The Consolidated Foods Case: A New Section
7 Test for the Conglomerate Merger," *Virginia Law Review*, XLIX (May,
1963), pp. 852, 864.

[72] Department of Justice complaint 1716 filed November 8, 1962. *U.S. v.
General Dynamics Corp.* (C.C.H., Cases Instituted in 1962, paragraph
45,062). Pending.

[73] C.C.H., Cases Instituted in 1962, paragraph 45,062, p. 52,503.

of products including nuclear-powered submarines, aircraft, and guided missiles; also telephonic, sound, and radar equipment, electric motors and generators, coal, concrete, and building materials. It is a heavy user of carbon dioxide. The company annually purchases more than $1 billion in goods from suppliers and in addition subcontracts out a substantial amount of the defense business to other producers.[74]

The government contended in part that acquisition of the largest manufacturer and distributor of carbon dioxide in the U.S. permitted General Dynamics to exercise extensive economic leverage to require suppliers and contractors to purchase carbon dioxide from its Liquid Carbonic Division, to the exclusion of independent suppliers of carbon dioxide. Liquid's competitive advantage over other manufacturers and distributors would continue to be enhanced because of actual and potential foreclosures of competitors from opportunities to compete.

SUMMARY AND CONCLUSIONS

Emphases in the cases

The Federal Trade Commission and the Department of Justice in their conglomerate-merger actions appear to have used three major theories of effects—wealth theory, potential-competition theory, and reciprocity theory. The wealth theory generally is based on some type of intrafirm resource shifting, in the cases reviewed, a subsidization of the acquired firm with certain resources of the acquiring firm. In this theory, the rational manager, in the expectation of eventual greater profits, subsidizes activities needing economic assistance. We may deduce from the cases at hand that resource-shifting is a common behavior pattern in conglomerate mergers regardless of the degree of node commonality. However, the particular form of subsidization depends on the degree of commonality. For example, in mergers of high node

---

[74] *Ibid.*, p. 52,504.

commonality—such as Procter and Gamble-Clorox—the sub-sidization frequently takes the form of joint-promotion and joint-distribution assistance, whereas in low-commonality mergers the assistance is more in the nature of pure financial transfers.

The wealth theory embraces most of the economic arguments leveled against conglomerate mergers in the Congressional hearings and reports before the 1950 amendment. There are far more variations to this theory than there are for the other two theories of effects.

Elimination of potential competition is at issue in the second theory. Mergers between firms in separate product markets as well as between firms in separate geographic markets are included. This theory may be termed "structural" in that its implications inhere in the fact that a potential competitor is eliminated. Consequently the implications may be evaluated immediately upon consummation of the merger.

Reciprocity is the third major theory used by the agencies in the conglomerate-merger actions. The agencies hold that conglomerate mergers may have both considerable structural opportunity as well as substantial persuasive power for reciprocity. Reciprocity frequently is occasioned by no more than a recognition of mutual benefit. It may, however, be effected through the persuasive power of a large-volume conglomerate buyer on potential and extant suppliers.

The mere possibility of reciprocity does not necessarily mean automatic implementation. There are reasons why the long-run profit-maximizing firm may decide against engaging in it. For instance, a firm may experience high opportunity costs by being committed to certain sources of supply regardless of the associated "guaranteed" sales, perhaps because lower quality of service and product may be supplied when sales are made to a "captive" account or because of a wish to avoid loss of goodwill if current customers and suppliers are replaced through reciprocity. Thus, the implications of the reciprocity issue are more difficult to ascertain than the implications of the other two theories.

Node commonality

Few mergers challenged by the administrative agencies were "pure" conglomerate mergers—that is, those approaching zero node commonality. Even in the dairy mergers, the commonality was relatively high, for the physical products of the acquired firms were frequently identical to those of the acquiring firm. Accordingly, purchasing, promotional, and managerial commonalities were probably present.

In virtually all conglomerate-merger cases in the potential-competition category, the node commonality was high. In most potential-competition cases where the government contended that the entry into the potential product market was negated, there were concomitant references to the potential economies inherent in the merger. The product-extension wealth-theory cases also exhibited high node commonality.

Post-acquisition data

What should be the role of post-acquisition data in assessing conglomerate mergers? The cases provide no consistent evidence on this issue.

One of the significant elements in the Commission decision in Procter & Gamble-Clorox is the denial of the necessity or applicability of post-acquisition data in conglomerate-merger cases.

> Admission of post-acquisition data is proper only in the unusual case in which the structure of the market has changed radically since the merger—for example, where the market share of the merged firm has dwindled to insignificance—or in the perhaps still more unusual case in which the adverse effects of the merger have already become manifest in the behavior of the firms in the market.[75]

According to the FTC view in Procter and Gamble-Clorox, post-acquisition evidence rarely has probative value. The Commission said that in passing Section 7, Congress postu-

---

[75] *Procter & Gamble Co.*, p. 21,560.

lated that certain kinds of market structure would lead to noncompetitive behavior. Thus if a market structure strongly suggesting anticompetitive effects is shown to have been created or aggravated by a merger, it is unnecessary to await the behavioral manifestations.[76]

If post-acquisition data are to be allowed any broader role in Section 7 proceedings, a respondent, so long as the merger is the subject of an investigation or proceeding, may deliberately refrain from anticompetitive conduct—may sheathe, as it were, the market power conferred by the merger—and build, instead, a record of good behavior to be used in rebuttal in the proceeding.[77]

On the other hand, in a conglomerate-merger case where reciprocity is the issue, a Court of Appeals was favorably disposed to the use of post-acquisition data:

And here ten years of post-acquisition experience—during which Consolidated attempted overt enforcement of reciprocal buying practice where it deemed it might be successful—serves to demonstrate that neither the acquisition of Gentry, in and of itself, nor the overt attempts to use buying power to influence sellers to Consolidated to purchase from Gentry resulted in substantial anti-competitive effect. [Consolidated's dehydrated-onion market share increased by some 7 percent since acquisition, while during the same period, its dehydrated-garlic market share decreased by approximately 12 percent.][78]

---

[76] *Ibid.*

[77] *Ibid.*, p. 21,574.

[78] *Consolidated Foods* v. *FTC* (C.C.H. 1964 Trade Cases, paragraph 71,-054), p. 79,168. However, on April 28, 1965, the U.S. Supreme Court reversed the Court of Appeals' ruling, acknowledging the occasional necessity for post-acquisition data but also stressing the interest of Section 7 in *probable* effects. (C.C.H. Trade Regulation Reporter, paragraph 71,432), p. 80,870. See also the statement by Justice Stewart in a concurring opinion, *ibid.*, p. 80,872. For other U.S. Supreme Court statements about the concern of Congress with probabilities, not certainties, in the framework of Section 7, see *Brown Shoe Co.* v. *U.S.* (370 U.S. 294, 323), and *U.S.* v. *Philadelphia National Bank* (374 U.S. 321, 362).

In view of the ambiguities and anomalies encountered in the attempt to assess the applicability of post-acquisition data, and with the clear Section-7 mandate of Congress as to probabilities, not certainties, the economist may contribute to clarification of this issue by developing predictive models. These models would assume managerial behavior based largely on the desire for economic gain. And with such predictive models, the inquiry will be able to avoid post-acquisition data and to deal only with factors pertinent in establishing reasonable inferences as to probable effect.[79]

---

[79] See Edward S. Mason, *Economic Concentration and the Monopoly Problem* (New York: Atheneum, 1964), pp. 392–395.

Chapter VI

SOURCES AND
IMPLEMENTATION OF
CONGLOMERATE MARKET POWER

IN SOME legislative hearings and reports on the Section-7 amendment it was contended that conglomerate firms possessed market capabilities superior to single-market or smaller firms. The cases in the preceding chapter also pointed up charges about the market abilities of conglomerate firms. This chapter will deal primarily with the "conglomerate market power" which may exist in a conglomerate firm—what it is, how and when it develops, what conditions determine its magnitude, and how it is implemented in a firm's market behavior.

The three theories about the effects of conglomerate mergers on competition set forth in Chapter V are not equally important in considering conglomerate market power, or in general, the behavior of conglomerates that may affect competition. Thus, the potential competition issue, which centers on structural change, is not pertinent. Reciprocity, too, depends in large part on structural opportunities; but there are also behavioral implications, and these to an extent fall within the range of our interest in this chapter's analysis of conglomerate behavior. However, the issue most critical in understanding how a conglomerate firm may generate superior market capabilities—and the one which will be most emphasized in this chapter—is wealth. Because of its many variations, the wealth theory contains numerous behavioral implications that merit attention.

DEFINITION OF CONGLOMERATE MARKET POWER

Conglomerate market power is the ability of a conglomerate firm at its discretion to shift marketing emphasis and resources among its markets and activities. The greater the ability for discretionary shifting of marketing emphasis and resources, the greater is the conglomerate market power.

Conglomerate market power is largely the consequence of rational managerial behavior. No value judgment inheres in the mere presence of conglomerate market power, whatever its magnitude. Nor—as will be shown—can one draw valid inferences as to effects on competition by looking only at the presence and magnitude of conglomerate market power.

THE SOURCES OF CONGLOMERATE MARKET POWER

The concept of conglomerate market power, as discussed here, is a basic part of the wealth theory. It was essentially wealth-theory arguments raised by the Federal Trade Commission and by various Congressmen which helped lead to the inclusion of conglomerate mergers in the 1950 amendment.

The central issue in the wealth theory was stated in two comments cited earlier concerning the alleged capabilities of the conglomerate firm. The Federal Trade Commission observed in a 1947 report: "Threatened with competition in any one of its fields of enterprise, the conglomerate corporation may sell below cost or may use other unfair methods in that field, absorbing its losses through excessive profits made in its other lines of activity."[1] And in 1949 hearings on monopoly, Dr. John M. Blair, Chief, Division of Economics, Bureau of Industrial Economics, Federal Trade Commission, testified:

---

[1] U.S., Congress, *The Present Trend of Corporate Mergers and Acquisitions,* Document 17, 8oth Cong., 1st Sess., 1947, pp. 12–13.

The Commission feels that the conglomerate type of acquisition is . . . peculiarly dangerous to small business. A company that is so diversified is in a position to strike out with great force against any smaller company which may seek to compete with it in any one of the variety of fields in which it is engaged and, of course, it is able to make up whatever losses that are incurred in the competitive war with its profits secured in the other fields in which it is engaged.[2]

In each of the wealth-theory cases discussed in Chapter V it was contended that the acquired firm was in some form subsidized by the acquiring firm. The wealth theory implies that rational managerial behavior in the merged entity will subsidize products and activities in the expectation of eventual increased profits. The wealth theory also implies that subsidization might be directed *from* the acquired firm to parts of the acquiring firm's operations. The issue, then, is the ability of the conglomerate firm to shift resources among its markets.

Discretionary power and the shifting of resources

In traditional price theory, a single-product firm has some degree of discretionary power if it has market power.[3] How does the conglomerate firm obtain discretionary power? In the short run, the conglomerate firm with sizable liquid assets is afforded considerable discretion in its market activities. But in the long run, in the absence of some sustaining sources of excess resources and the ability to focus on any market, a stock of liquid assets will be completely dissipated. What,

---

[2] U.S., Congress, House, Subcommittee of the Committee on the Judiciary, *Hearings on Study of Monopoly Power*, 82nd Cong., 1st Sess., 1949, Serial No. 14, Part 1, pp. 219–220.

[3] Market power or monopoly power is some protection from a competitive forcing of prices toward short-run marginal costs. It is the ability of the firm to behave persistently in a manner different from the behavior that a competitive market would enforce on a firm facing otherwise similar cost and demand conditions. See Edward S. Mason, *Economic Concentration and the Monopoly Problem* (New York: Atheneum, 1964), p. 93, and Carl Kaysen and Donald F. Turner, *Antitrust Policy* (Cambridge: Harvard University Press, 1959), p. 75.

then, are long-run sustaining sources of at least some discretionary power and at least some amount of shiftable (excess) resources? To answer that question, we must first ask: "For what conglomerate firms is the notion of shifting resources even relevant?"

For a firm in the long run to have excess resources to employ as it chooses, its total revenue must exceed its total costs—that is, to earn greater than normal profits. This is not to say that all solvent conglomerate firms (revenues at least equal costs including normal profits) have some degree of conglomerate market power. For some long-run solvent firms, the exact condition of total revenues equaling total costs may hold. Even such a firm, or even, logically, a temporarily insolvent firm, may have a type of conglomerate market power if there are profit imbalances among its various markets *and* if it is phasing out some current activities and entering new ones. This, however, is a special case. The condition of total revenue exceeding total costs is the far more significant case, for it affords considerable discretionary power for focusing on *any* current or new market.

Now, how probable is it that a conglomerate firm has total revenue exceeding total costs including normal profit? TR equals TC in two circumstances: either each of the firm's markets yields exactly a normal profit, or the excess profits earned in some markets exactly offset the losses experienced elsewhere. In an uncertain world, these balances are highly unlikely. More specifically, in a world in which different competitive conditions exist in the conglomerate firm's markets, perfect market adjustments for the firm as a whole are unlikely and the probability of exactly normal profits in all markets or exactly equal offsets of profits and losses is very low. On the other hand, long-run total revenues less than total costs contradicts the solvent-firm definition. Hence a greater-than-normal profits situation of total revenue exceeding total costs is most likely for a solvent conglomerate.

Additional support for expecting total revenue to exceed total costs in a conglomerate firm can be reasoned from the character of the conglomerate. A firm having several markets has more information on additional profit opportunities than a single-market firm. In time, through learning, it can better direct its search for profitable new opportunities. It is also able to be a more efficient allocator of capital not only because it can select ever-better sets of profitable alternatives but, because of its broader base of information, it can also better select the best alternative among the opportunities. The chosen alternative, in turn, suggests additional alternatives; and so on. All in all, then, it appears that the solvent conglomerate will typically have at least some measure of conglomerate market power.

Where do net over-all excess resources come from? Certainly the condition of total revenues exceeding total costs *could* hold in the absence of market power in any market. In such a case the inequality between total revenue and total costs would be due to random short-run windfall circumstances such as sudden outward demand shifts. Although such windfall situations could adventitiously persist among the conglomerate's markets in the long run, the probability of such good fortune persisting over time must be considered very small. Thus, it is market power itself, in the conglomerate firm's markets, that leads in net to the firm's total revenue exceeding total costs and hence to the at least minimal amount of conglomerate market power in virtually all solvent conglomerates.[4]

---

[4] This conclusion runs counter to another school of thought, enunciated primarily by Corwin Edwards. He argues that power can be derived from diversified bigness even in the absence of market control—largely through nonmarket leverages. Edwards' arguments are compelling for short-run phenomena; however, in the absence of market power, it would seem that the nonmarket and market manifestations of this power would eventually not be self-sustaining.

See Corwin D. Edwards, "Conglomerate Bigness as a Source of Power," *Business Concentration and Price Policy*, National Bureau of Economic Research (Princeton: Princeton University Press, 1955). Others have questioned as well whether there is anything beyond the purview of monopoly theory in Edwards' conglomerate. See George W. Stocking, "Comment on 'Conglomerate Bigness as a Source of Power'," *ibid.*, pp. 352–359. Also see George Stigler, "Mergers and Preventive Antitrust Policy," *University of Pennsylvania*

The rationale of intrafirm shifting follows, as was intimated earlier, from the fact that the firm seeks profit. The firm allocates its resources among its activities in accordance with the expected value in terms of profits. For example, in the short run a conglomerate firm may sustain an unprofitable plant from the earnings of other activities; but this occurs only in the expectation of eventual profits from those activities and of the consequent increase in total-firm profits. Simply stated, rational managerial behavior in a conglomerate firm is that of "global" maximization.[5]

Whether the particular shifting decisions are "correct" from either a managerial or social standpoint is not at issue here. The important point for this study is that considerable discretionary power may be available to the decision makers, however well or poorly it is used. As noted earlier, the conglomerate firm may indeed be a highly efficient allocator of capital to its most productive uses. It must simultaneously assess the marginal efficiency of capital on many fronts, and hence it may make investment decisions with more confidence of their relative profitability than can single-market firms. By the same token, conglomerate firms may impede allocation of resources by interposing the conglomerate firm's decision makers as intermediaries between the investing public and the various possible fields of investment.[6]

Law Review, CIV (1955), p. 184, John M. Blair, "The Conglomerate Merger in Economics and Law," The Georgetown Law Journal, XCVI (Summer, 1958), p. 685; and William Lee Baldwin, Antitrust and the Changing Corporation (Durham: Duke University Press, 1961), p. 225.

[5] For additional support and evidence that individual products, markets, and prices are not considered in isolation in conglomerate firms but that price and nonprice policies are set with an eye to total firm profits, see David Schwartzman, "Multiple-Company Mergers and the Theory of the Firm," Oxford Economic Papers, New Series, VII (June, 1955), pp. 197 ff.; Robert F. Lanzillotti, "Pricing Objectives in Large Companies," American Economic Review, XLVIII (December, 1958), p. 939; and Edwards, op. cit., p. 332.

In a statement that underscores the global-decision nature of the conglomerate firm, Clark has called the shifting of resources the "dominant and individualizing characteristic of the conglomerate firm." Richard C. Clark, "Conglomerate Mergers and Section 7 of the Clayton Act," Notre Dame Lawyer, XXXVI (May, 1961), p. 272.

[6] Jesse Markham, "Merger Policy Under the New Section 7: A Six Year

Additional shiftable resources

Shiftable resources beyond the minimal amounts commonly found in nonfailing conglomerate firms may arise in conglomerate firms. One source is market power which by definition results in excess profits—an increase in market power increases the resources that may be shifted within the firm. But there is also another fundamental source of shiftable resources, namely increased efficiency resulting from the absorption of excess capacity.

The role of excess capacity has been repeatedly underscored as perhaps the most important inducement for growth in a firm and specifically for diversification. If a conglomerate merger leads to fuller use of the capacity of either the acquiring or acquired firm, then efficiencies result. The savings can provide additional employable funds for internal shifting. As was pointed out in Chapter IV, excess capacity can best be used in mergers with high node commonality; and although virtually all viable conglomerate firms have some employable resources and discretionary power, those with high node commonality may by absorbing excess capacity develop substantial employable resources.

MARKET TACTICS

The shifting of resources within a conglomerate firm may take many forms. In low-node-commonality mergers the shifting may take the form of a financial subsidy of a particular product. Mergers with a higher degree of commonality may lead to more functional shifting such as joint promotional campaigns and joint branding and joint distribution of products.

Whatever the form of the tactics, the significance for a

Appraisal," *Virginia Law Review*, XLIII (May, 1957), pp. 498–499. See also Mason's interesting article on "managerial capitalism" being substituted for decentralized decision-making, the traditional hallmark of a market economy. E. S. Mason, "The Apologetics of 'Managerialism'," *The Journal of Business*, XXXI (January, 1958).

conglomerate merger is that the shifting provides some part of the firm with marketing possibilities beyond those previously existing. With excess resources most abundant in mergers with high node commonality, the greatest number of types of tactics or magnitude of tactics are, accordingly, available in these firms. Thus, in high-node-commonality mergers, in period t_1 there may be many opportunities for absorption of excess capacity. In period t_2 funds generated from the efficiencies constitute additional employable resources. Excess capacity is a continually recurring phenomenon; hence the two-stage process constitutes a never-ending cycle. The greater the absorption of excess capacity, the greater the shiftable resources. This is why the number and magnitude of feasible market tactics are in direct proportion to the degree of node commonality in the conglomerate firm.

If shifted resources are to increase profits, the conglomerate firm usually must possess a "staying ability" that allows it to outlast its rivals. This staying ability appears to derive from the same determinants as those which contribute to conglomerate market power. That is, in the short run, staying ability is, in effect, simply a function of liquid assets. But in the long run it is a function of profits or cost savings from elsewhere in the firm. Thus, staying ability tends to vary with degree of node commonality between the acquiring and acquired firms or with market power in the firm. (It may be argued that a small firm acquired by a much larger firm will enjoy staying ability. However, in the absence of a sustainable flow of resources such as high node commonality and market power provide, the size discrepancy provides only a short-run staying ability.)

Advertising and price-cutting

Two frequently discussed tactics are advertising and price-cutting. Advertising is rational in a profit-seeking firm only if the product, offering, or establishment is potentially differentiable in one or more markets. Price-cutting, of course, is conceivable whether differentiation is possible or not. The important point about price-cutting in the context of conglomerate market power is that the conglomerate firm may cut some of its prices even to below-cost levels. Short-run losses can be offset by excess profits elsewhere in the firm. Or, as we have pointed out, losses may be offset by resources generated through the absorption of excess capacity.

Advertising is one of the most effective ways in which a conglomerate firm can "reflect" its market power in entering a new market. In general, a high degree of conglomerate market power enables the diversifying firm to undertake a long and intensive advertising campaign in the geographic or product markets it is entering. As a result, the buyers in the new industry may be made forcefully aware of the firm whose reputation in other industries is well established. Moreover, the "closer" the new markets are to the extant ones, the greater will be the effectiveness per advertising dollar because in general the greater will be the brand awareness.

Reciprocity

Degree of node commonality is critical for reciprocity, too. Reciprocity does not depend, however, upon conglomerate market power potentially to affect competition, for it does not involve shifting of resources in the wealth-theory sense. In contrast to the wealth factor, reciprocity is only negligibly concerned with market power of sellers. It is based more on the *significance* of a firm as a purchaser of products whose suppliers are also potential customers of the purchaser's products. Reciprocal purchasing by firms may be simply the result of tacit "mutual-dependence-recognized" behavior. It is possible, however, that if the buyer is both large in general and is a large purchaser of the particular products of another (especially a smaller) firm, the latter may feel "compelled" to purchase, if at all possible, from the large customer.

There are several important implications of diversification for effecting reciprocity; and, as we shall see, there is significant variation in the kinds of diversified firms that can best employ this frequently advantageous tactic.[7] Clearly, the primary economic significance of reciprocity is that a firm is often enabled to make sales that it could not otherwise make or could make only at greater costs. How, specifically, does diversification bear upon reciprocity?

Clearly, a would-be participant in reciprocity must find a potential buyer of its goods among extant and potential suppliers of the goods it buys. By definition, a diversified firm operates in more than one product or geographic market. Thus, a diversified firm has more reciprocal buying opportunities than an equal-sized single-market firm. (The latter can on occasion effect triangular arrangements, but they are usually inconvenient and risky.) Diversification often not only increases the number of opportunities for reciprocity, but may increase their magnitude as well. By diversifying into products requiring the same input as its old products, a firm enlarges its potential reciprocity by being able to exert greater economic pressure on suppliers who are potential buyers. Thus, for instance, if there is much production-node commonality in the diversification, the quantity of the inputs may be substantially increased. To that extent, reciprocity based on inputs is enhanced. In general, many of a large conglomerate's purchases of goods and services may provide means of increasing sales. For example, even advertising accounts, which are likely to be relatively small for firms engaged in industrial marketing, may aggregate such large sums as to give the advertiser leverage in obtaining business.[8]

---

[7] Many ideas in this section are derived from George W. Stocking and Willard F. Mueller, "Business Reciprocity and the Size of Firms," *The Journal of Business*, XXX (April, 1957). Determining what reciprocity may mean to *competition* in the market involves consideration of variables beyond the mere existence of reciprocity. Chapter VII provides a discussion of the most important of those variables.

[8] *Ibid.*, p. 77. As a case in point, DuPont in 1935 was able to bring pressure on the Curtis Publishing Company to get business from a supplier of one of its affiliates. See *ibid.* text at nn. 46–47.

Reciprocity has on occasion been used for everything from (1) collusive dividing of markets to lessen the severity of competition; (2) to ensuring an adequate supply of an essential raw material in time of shortage; and (3) to expanding sales without resorting to price competition. However, it is the

The diversified's firm's greater reciprocity opportunities arise not only because of its own spread over more than one market, but also because, given the ubiquity of diversification among industrial firms, it deals with conglomerate firms. When a conglomerate firm with a low degree of node commonality confronts numerous suppliers each of which is highly diversified, the opportunities for direct or complex reciprocal relationships can be numerous indeed. And, as has been shown, the large concentrated or aggregated purchases frequently possible in conglomerate firms may provide opportunities to tie up large sales volumes.

SUMMARY

Conglomerate market power is the ability of a conglomerate firm at its discretion to shift marketing emphasis and resources among its markets and activities. The greater the ability for discretionary shifting of marketing emphasis and resources, the greater the conglomerate market power. Some conglomerate market power (perhaps minimal) exists in virtually *all* solvent conglomerate firms. Additional conglomerate market power, which is to say, discretionary power and additional shiftable resources, is generated both externally and internally. Externally, it is created through increased market power in one or some of the conglomerate firm's markets. Internally, additional shiftable resources are generated through the absorption of excess capacity.

Given the freedom to focus on any market of its choosing, and given resources to employ in any market, a conglomerate firm's management *will* shift resources among the firm's markets and activities because it is trying to maximize long-run total profits. Thus, resources are allocated in accordance with the expected value of profits from their employment. Fre-

---

power of reciprocal buying to increase a firm's sales that is most significant to industrial structure. For example, Armour & Company used its buying power to persuade railroads to buy equipment made by its subsidiary, the Waugh Equipment Company. "Within only six years after Armour acquired Waugh, it had risen from sixth place in the industry to first, while total industry sales were declining." *Ibid.*, p. 94.

quently products suffering losses will be subsidized, so to speak, by profits made elsewhere in the conglomerate. However, the subsidization of losses from products or plants will occur only insofar as the firm can thereby envisage increased total profits in the long run.

The shifting of the resources takes many forms, the particular form being, in large part, a function of the degree of node commonality. In low-node-commonality firms, the form of the internal transfer will frequently be purely financial. In high-node-commonality firms, the implementation of the transfer appears in more functional forms, for example, joint promotion and joint distribution of products through common channels of distribution.

To achieve the firm's market goals, the internal shifting must frequently be continued for some time. This "staying ability" in pursuit of certain ends through internal subsidizations, derives from the same sources as conglomerate market power. Thus, one may simply say that a firm with high conglomerate market power has a proportionate amount of staying ability.

Reciprocity is a second market-behavior type in conglomerate mergers. For different reasons, the degree of node commonality is seen to be as strategic to implications for reciprocity as it was for implications for conglomerate market power. For example, with high-node-commonality diversification, the average sales per reciprocity arrangement could be very large because of the large purchasing leverage afforded by the commonality. On the other hand, low-node-commonality diversification may provide fewer large-volume reciprocity arrangements, but increases the number of reciprocity opportunities in general. This is due not only to the conglomerate firm itself being highly diversified, but also to the fact that the firm frequently is buying from conglomerate firms similarly highly diversified. Thus, the likelihood is large, in such cases, that the former will find products that it can sell on a reciprocal basis to its suppliers.

The concept of conglomerate market power is a part of

the wealth theory. Conglomerate market power emerges from the analysis as something that might be called "a *potential* ability to affect competition." The greater the conglomerate market power, the greater the potential ability to affect competition. We have seen that in addition to extant market strength, it is precisely those conglomerate mergers that are most rational in terms of efficient use of resources, i.e., high node commonality, that are the mergers with the greatest potential to affect competition. But we stress that to determine the probable effect of a conglomerate merger on competition, it is not enough merely to look at the amount of conglomerate market power in the merger. All relevant factors in interaction will suggest the probable effect.

Chapter VII

THE COMPETITIVE
EFFECTS OF
CONGLOMERATE MERGERS

WE can now confront the main question of this study: "Under what conditions and in what direction may conglomerate mergers affect competition?"

Let us understand competition to be the active rivalry of firms for customers in a market. The remainder of this discussion will attempt to delineate the situations in which conglomerate mergers are most likely to affect competition, particularly by means of conglomerate market power, and to indicate tools both for appraising conglomerate mergers and statements made about the ability of conglomerate mergers to affect competition.

As Chapter III indicated, the amended Section 7 is concerned with the *probable* competitive effect of mergers. But "competition" as it appears in real markets is not a simple concept. Few economists can completely agree on the amount of competition in a particular market, and by how much it may be lessened or strengthened by changes in that market. Economists do agree generally that the structure of the market importantly conditions the behavior of the firms in that market, at least in polar cases. Thus, a change in one or more key structural elements may well lead to a change in the character of competitive behavior in the market. Also, a change in the nature of one of the market participants, as possibly from a conglomerate merger, may change competitive behavior. In a dynamic context, then, structure tends to condition behavior, and behavior may have effects on structure. The present analysis will not attempt to assess the absolute level of competition in a market; it will focus on the factors in conglomerate mergers making for a probable change in the level of competition and will also focus on the direction of the change. In so doing we encounter all the complexity and controversy associated with the issue of the competitive effects of conglomerate mergers.

Clark posed a worthy goal for the analysis of conglomerate mergers: "Those conglomerate mergers exhibiting no anticompetitive consequences must be classified and differentiated from acquisitions that produce substantial competitive deterioration."[1] Controversy arises because, according to some, such differentiation is not required or is not possible. On the one hand, the hearings and reports on the amendment to Section 7 strongly indicated that conglomerate mergers were to be considered in large part inherently anticompetitive. It was repeatedly argued that conglomerate mergers in virtually all cases served to lessen competition. In this view, automatic "elimination of potential competition" or the frequent opportunities for reciprocity that result from a conglomerate merger *ipso facto* lessen competition. On the other hand, there is Adelman's statement: "The fact is that a truly conglomerate merger cannot be attacked in order to maintain competition, because it has no effect on any market structure."[2]

This study questions both of these extreme views. The position taken by the FTC and others in the hearings and reports on the amendment is clear enough and has been amply discussed in earlier chapters. However, we might consider several aspects of Adelman's view in greater detail. A "truly conglomerate merger" can be defined as a conglomerate merger with very low node commonality. This would virtually be a pure investment merger. But conglomerate mergers

---

[1] Richard C. Clark, "Conglomerate Mergers and Section 7 of the Clayton Act," *Notre Dame Lawyer*, XXXVI (May, 1961), p. 267.

[2] M. A. Adelman, "The Anti-Merger Act, 1950–1960," *American Economic Review*, LI (May, 1961), p. 243.

with very low node commonality are the exception. However, it is not because of the infrequency of this type of merger that Adelman claims they do not affect market structure. He appears to be arguing that their lack of effect on market structure follows from their "truly conglomerate" character.

To be sure, as for levels of concentration and of barriers to entry, *no* conglomerate merger *per se* affects structure—whether the merger has high or low commonality. At the time it is consummated the merger is merely a transfer of control. Nevertheless, even though conglomerate mergers, unlike horizontal and vertical mergers, do not affect market structure at the time of transfer of title, under certain conditions they may affect market structure subsequently. Accordingly, they may affect competition. Furthermore, our analysis suggests that even the "truly conglomerate" (pure investment) merger can have an effect on market structure and hence on competition. The mere possibility of an effect is, of course, not enough; but the framework also suggests the likelihood of such effects.

CONGLOMERATE MERGERS, MARKET STRUCTURE, AND COMPETITIVE IMPLICATIONS

Because this analysis deals primarily with market-structure effects, it is necessary to comment on the nature of market structure and the length to which, given changes in key structural variables, one can infer changes in competition. Market structure embodies the framework, conditioning environment, or situation within which the behavior of enterprises takes place. Behavior (encompassing both the market conduct and market performance of firms) is strategically influenced by certain characteristics of the organization of the market.[3]

The structural characteristics most frequently emphasized as strategic are: (1) degree of seller concentration (described by the number and size distribution of sellers in the market);

---

[3] Joe S. Bain, *Industrial Organization* (New York: Wiley, 1959), p. 266.

(2) degree of buyer concentration (described by the number and size distribution of buyers in the market); (3) degree of product differentiation among the outputs of the various sellers (defined as the extent to which the outputs are viewed as nonidentical by buyers); and (4) condition of entry to the market (defined as the relative ease or difficulty with which new sellers may enter the market, and determined generally by the advantages which established sellers have over potential entrants).[4]

Which of the structure variables are the most important as determinants of behavior? Bain's research suggests that the structure variables most critically associated with the profit dimension of performance are degree of seller concentration and condition of entry into the market. Seller concentration and condition of entry in combination *and* separately influence the profit dimension of performance. The degree of product differentiation is significant also, but its effect is probably felt most strongly in determining the height of the entry barriers.[5] According to Bain, product differentiation is the source of the highest barriers to entry; scale economies and absolute-cost advantages are second and third, respectively, as important sources of barriers.[6] On the basis of Bain's findings plus a general consensus among economists on the importance of the level of concentration and condition of entry, this analysis will focus primarily on the effects of conglomerate mergers on these variables, and particularly on the extent to which the mergers influence already moderate-to-high seller concentration and barrier levels. Because Bain found a strong correlation between high levels of concentration and barriers (separately and in combination) and monopolistic excess profits, we shall limit our analysis to situations in which concentration and barrier levels are already moderate-to-high. The degree of buyer concentra-

---

[4] *Ibid.*, pp. 7–8.
[5] *Ibid.*, Chapter 10.
[6] *Ibid.*, pp. 248–253.

tion in Bain's study did not appear to be as significant a determinant of market behavior, and in order to avoid unimportant complications we will assume a constant, low-to-moderate degree of buyer concentration.

To what extent may structural changes be considered as tantamount to changes in level of competition? Generally, the plane of competition cannot be inferred directly and exclusively from data relating to the structure of the market, for most markets do not closely approach the only two models—pure competition and pure monopoly—under which equilibrium conditions permit inferences of behavior from structure. Also, such clear-cut predictive models are static, not dynamic. Thus, important as structural data are, market-power evidence can really be found only in the combined study of market structure and business behavior.[7] However, this view does not negate the informational value of changes in the structure variables. While changes in structure cannot tell us by how much competition may have changed, they may well suggest the *direction* of change in the level of competition. Let us recall that the analysis of merger effects under Section 7 is concerned with future probabilities and not ex-post facts. Indeed, it is for this reason that Kaysen and Turner say in regard to Section 7, as contrasted to the Sherman Act: "In particular, much more reliance would have to be placed on *structural* evidence, since behavioral evidence would normally be available only for the market as it existed in the past."[8] Therefore, it is appropriate to infer competitive implications from probable changes in structure. In doing so, this analysis is, moreover, protected from overstatement because it emphasizes cases with a high probability of changes in the key structure variables. Accordingly, the probability of change in the level of competition is certainly not insignificant.

---

[7] Edward S. Mason in Preface to Carl Kaysen and Donald F. Turner, *Antitrust Policy* (Cambridge: Harvard University Press, 1959), pp. xviii-xix.

[8] *Ibid.*, pp. 132–133, emphasis added.

The most significant feature of a conglomerate merger able to affect market structure clearly is conglomerate market power—in particular, a high magnitude of conglomerate market power. If there is in the conglomerate firm a magnitude of conglomerate market power higher than that of most competitors in the market, then the merger affords relatively clear implications for structural effects. For reasons stated in Chapters IV and VI, we would expect the magnitude of conglomerate market power to increase in time as management both learned through experience (and hence improved its resource allocation) and effected increased commonalities to attain efficiencies. Such behavior would be normal within the framework of the long-run profit-maximizing goal. But of greatest relevance to Section-7 inquiry is the question: "What *at the time of the merger* can be said about the probable effects on competition?" Mergers with a magnitude of conglomerate market power higher than that of most competitors permit the strongest inferences as of the time of the merger.

Three major factors explain why only a high magnitude of conglomerate market power is truly important for an analysis of probable effects: (1) Typically, firms enjoy and seek to expand a degree of product or enterprise differentiation; (2) typically, firms in the economy are multi-market (product or geographic) and hence may be expected to have some degree of conglomerate market power; (3) it is clear from observation that many markets are relatively concentrated, and some are highly concentrated; therefore, in the many markets characterized by differentiated oligopoly with at least some conglomerate market power, only a significant "shock" can have an appreciable effect on the level of concentration and condition of entry. Heflebower has pointed out the resiliency of differentiated oligopolies (with even greater resiliency if we add to them at least some conglomerate market power): "In general, the less the product and its market conform to the specifications for a pure oligopoly . . . the more likely it is that the important elements of the market positions of rivals will be such that they cannot be easily upset by feasible competitive devices."[9]

But in drawing inferences for competitive effects, are we justified in assuming that the high-magnitude conglomerate market power is implemented? Certainly, it is always possible that it could exist but not be used. We may, however, assume its implementation because we assume a goal of long-run profit maximization. Furthermore, under Section 7 we are interested in probable effects and not ex-post events. Many implications of conglomerate mergers would stay forever obscure if we did not assume long-run profit maximization and infer accordingly. For the vast majority of real world firms and markets, it is a reasonable assumption.

Since we are interested in probable effects on competition in a market, we must decide what market is relevant. Should the analysis focus on a market in the acquired firm, on a market in the acquiring firm, or on some potential new market? It will help to divide the answer into two parts: the relevant market in a real-world analysis of conglomerate market power, and a relevant market under the simplifying assumption used in this analysis. With respect to the first part, the concept of conglomerate market power and the shifting of resources suggests implications for *any* of the post-merger markets. For reasons developed in Chapter VI, the wealth theory can apply to the shifting of resources in either direction between the acquiring and acquired firms. The conglomerate is a global decision maker and two-way shifting is very likely. Two-way shifting is particularly probable when the excess resources in the acquired firm are significant relative to the needs of the acquiring firm, or, generally, when the difference of size between the firms is not too great. On the other hand, when a large firm acquires a much smaller firm, one would assume, in the short run at least, that more resources will be shifted

---

[9] Richard B. Heflebower, "Toward a Theory of Industrial Markets and Prices," reprinted in American Economic Association, *Readings in Industrial Organization and Public Policy* (Homewood, Illinois: Richard D. Irwin, 1958), p. 303.

into the smaller firm. The important point for the real-world analysis of conglomerate mergers is that resources *can* and *will* be shifted to whatever part of the conglomerate firm affords the greater long-run profit opportunities. The discussion will be clearer, however, if we assume the relevant market is one of the acquired firm's markets and that resources are shifted from the acquiring into the acquired firm.

CONGLOMERATE MARKET POWER

AND LESSENING OF COMPETITION

Increase in the Level of Concentration

Any conglomerate merger that may increase the level of concentration and barriers to entry, particularly above "moderate" levels, may lessen competition. If at the time of the merger, concentration or barriers are already at least "moderate," then a conglomerate merger that may increase these levels provides implications for a change in the level of competition.

How can a conglomerate merger increase the level of concentration in a market? How can a conglomerate merger enable the acquired firm (the special case for this analysis) to increase its market share either faster than the total market is growing or at the expense of smaller rivals? Clearly, if a firm improves its product or offering or increases its sales-promotion outlays more than its rivals at any given price, it is likely to increase its share of the market. Or if a firm offers its product or service at a lower price than its rivals, it creates a strong probability of increasing its share of the market. As we saw in Chapter VI, if the merged entity had *greater* conglomerate market power than any or most of the other firms, then it was better able, for example, to devote resources to product improvement or to persist in sales promotion activities longer than most of its rivals. In general, when a conglomerate has a high magnitude of conglomerate market power, that is, a magnitude higher than any or most firms in a particular market, then its ability to engage in competition is to the same degree greater than that of the less-powered firms. In these ways, then, a conglomerate merger affording a high magnitude of conglomerate market power, enables the acquired firm to gain in market share. What the increase in market share implies for effects on competition depends on the relative position of the acquired firm in its market and the level of concentration at the time of the merger. If the market is already moderately-to-highly concentrated and if the acquired firm is relatively large in its market, then the high magnitude of conglomerate market power will tend to increase the level of concentration in the market and to lessen competition.

We have so far been considering general, probable tendencies. Exceptions may, however, occur. It is always possible that, for example, the acquisition of a relatively large firm in an already moderately concentrated market may sharpen competitive forces, particularly in a highly interdependent oligopolistic market. With its newly increased conglomerate market power, the acquired firm might eschew marketing traditions and established price-leadership patterns, injecting a new element of uncertainty into the market. This is especially likely in global decision-making where a conflict develops between a conglomerate's national policy and the traditional behavior patterns in a particular market.[10] The acquired firm may, as we saw earlier, receive and benefit from the introduction of research results and innovations emanating from the conglomerate's other markets and activities. To the extent that the innovations developed and adopted by the merged entity are greater than those which would have been developed on its own, competition may be stimulated. However, *all* these events are equally likely whether the acquired firm is relatively large or small. Furthermore, a relatively large acquired firm in an already moderately-to-highly concentrated market, will in gaining a market share tend to increase con-

---

[10] See John M. Blair, "The Conglomerate Merger in Economics and Law," *The Georgetown Law Journal*, XLVI (Summer, 1958), pp. 692–693.

centration and thereby to decrease competition in the *long run*. Thus, while heightened competition among the large firms in a market is possible (not necessarily probable) because of the acquisition of a relatively large firm, such a merger, nevertheless, probably bodes ill for total market competition in the long run. Thus, we note again the important competitive implications of the relative position of the acquired firm.

We may summarize in a proposition the conditions wherein a conglomerate merger may tend to lessen competition by probably increasing the level of concentration:

Proposition I

Given that the acquired firm has a relatively high magnitude of conglomerate market power and that it is relatively large in an already moderately-to-highly concentrated market, it is probable that the merger will increase concentration and therefore will tend to lessen competition.

This proposition applies equally to differentiated and homogeneous goods and services. As discussed in Chapter VI, the manifestations of conglomerate market power take different forms in differentiated and undifferentiated markets. For example, the tactics of advertising and sales promotion are more appropriate in the differentiated market; whereas, price cutting is to be more expected in the homogeneous case. The manner in which the conglomerate market power is implemented is a function of the competitive possibilities as seen by the conglomerate firm's decision makers. The major difference between pure and differentiated oligopoly cases is that in pure oligopolies less "shock" is needed to alter the organization of the market.

Increase in Barriers to Entry

Any conglomerate merger that may substantially increase the level of barriers to entry, particularly above "moderate" levels, may lessen competition. Under some circumstances conglomerate mergers may increase barriers to entry, particularly product-differentiation barriers, which Bain found to be the highest barriers.

The sources of these barriers have a bearing on this situation. A product-differentiation barrier is an advantage of established firms over potential entrants because of the preference of buyers for the established firms and products. The sources of product-differentiation barriers are (1) the accumulated preferences of buyers (often by the influence of long-sustained advertising) for established brands and firms; (2) the exclusive control of superior product designs through patent protection; and (3) the control of favored distribution systems when alternative systems can be established, if at all, only at disadvantageous cost to the entrant firm.[11]

As we saw in Chapter VI, a high magnitude of conglomerate market power affords an ability to persist in promoting a product or service in any market. And high node commonality in the marketing activities of the acquired and acquiring firms can afford great awareness of the acquiring firm's brands in the markets of the acquired firm. Thus, the acquired firm's products benefit (a) from identification and joint promotion with the acquiring firm's products and brands which may already enjoy broad acceptance in their own markets; (b) from distribution along with some of the acquiring firm's products, implying a possible foreclosing for potential entrants of distributive alternatives in the acquired firm's market; and (c) from the mentioned staying ability implicit in a high magnitude of conglomerate market power enabling the acquiring firm to undertake sustained promotion of the acquired firm's products.

Still another implication also stems from high marketing commonality. The acquiring firm might logically add to the acquired firm's product line a competing product line, thereby stratifying the market in terms, for example, of quality and

---

[11] Bain, *op. cit.*, pp. 239–241.

price. Or, if the new brand is essentially of the same quality and price as the existing brand, the addition may fence in the "core" lines and thus discourage entry by confronting potential entrants with size, organization, and a variety of product offerings.[12]

How, then, shall we generalize about the probable ability of a conglomerate merger to increase product differentiation barriers? Given a differentiable product in the acquired firm, a high magnitude of conglomerate market power in the merger will tend to benefit the acquired firm's product. If the conglomerate market power stems primarily from market profits rather than from commonalities, the promotion of the product will be enhanced by the staying ability concomitant with high conglomerate market power. If the high conglomerate market power stems as much or more from marketing commonalities, the promotion of the acquired firm's product will be enhanced not only by the staying ability, but by intermarket awareness, joint-promotion possibilities, common-channel-of-distribution possibilities, and related marketing opportunities. (The Procter & Gamble-Clorox merger showed some of these characteristics.) Thus, the increased marketing possibilities enabled by the marketing commonalities and general high magnitude of conglomerate market power tend to heighten the preferences of buyers for the product of the acquired firm, as well as to create for the acquired firm a more dominant position in its channels of distribution.

Under what conditions, then, would all this lead to an increase in product-differentiation barriers? It would tend to increase these barriers if the acquired firm were relatively large in its market. And when might the increase in the level of product-differentiation barriers lessen competition? We would suggest the latter result when the existing level of these barriers was at least "moderate" at the time of the merger.

We may now summarize in two propositions the conditions

---

[12] See Robert F. Lanzillotti, "Multiple Products and Oligopoly Strategy: A Development of Chamberlin's Theory of Products," *Quarterly Journal of Economics*, LXVIII (August, 1954), p. 467.

in which a conglomerate merger may lessen competition by probably increasing the level of product-differentiation barriers to entry.

Proposition II

Given that the acquired firm has a differentiable product and a relatively high magnitude of conglomerate market power, and given that it is relatively large in a market with an already moderate-to-high level of product-differentiation barriers, it is probable that the merger will increase these barriers, and, therefore, will tend to lessen competition.

Proposition III

Given the same conditions as in Proposition II and given also that the high magnitude of conglomerate market power stems in large part from a high degree of marketing node commonality, it is probable that the merger will tend to raise the barriers higher than under the conditions of Proposition II.

There are also conditions under which a conglomerate merger may substantially increase scale-economy barriers, which, according to Bain, are the second-highest barrier. The barrier resulting from economies of large-scale production and distribution means that the entrant must supply a significant fraction of the total industry output in order to attain lowest average unit costs. The entrant encounters a similar phenomenon if there are advantages of large-scale promotion, such that a firm must be large enough to supply a significant fraction of industry output in order to gain the best ratio of unit selling price to unit sales-promotion cost.[13]

It was apparent in Chapter IV that considerable efficiency opportunities exist in conglomerate mergers of high node commonality. For example, if the merger facilitates common production processes and raw materials for the acquiring and acquired firms, and also makes it possible for the products to be promoted and distributed jointly, substantial economies

---

[13] Bain, *op. cit.*, p. 241.

may be realized. If real economies of scale are possible, such as in distribution, then a conglomerate merger with high marketing node commonality could probably attain them. If the economies are attainable only at a high output level, and if the acquired firm is relatively large in its market, then a merger with high marketing node commonality may not merely achieve the economies but may also exert upward pressure on the level of these barriers. The increase in the level of scale-economy barriers may be said to lessen competition when the earlier level of these barriers was already moderate to high. We may summarize scale-economy barriers in a fourth proposition; but in so doing we should recognize that these barriers were deemed by Bain to be less significant than product-differentiation barriers:

Proposition IV

Given that the acquired firm has a relatively high magnitude of conglomerate market power stemming primarily from a high degree of production or marketing node commonality, and given that it is relatively large in a market with an already moderate-to-high level of scale-economy barriers, it is probable that the merger will increase these barriers, and therefore, will tend to lessen competition.

Frequently, the economies can be attained at merely moderate output levels, but, on occasion, they can be attained only at very high levels of output. The Procter & Gamble-Clorox case is an example of the latter. Through marketing-node commonalities, the merger enabled Clorox to "save" $138,500 on advertising for a twelve-month period.[14] Thus, any potential entrant into Clorox's market, unless the potential entrant is very large, must consider the significantly enlarged disadvantage of promotion economies. In the Procter & Gamble-Clorox situation, it is particularly noteworthy that Clorox was the largest national marketer of liquid bleach, with about 50 percent of the market. Yet, it was still not pos-

---

[14] See Chapter V, n. 10, above, and accompanying text.

sible for it to attain the volume discount on advertising until it established marketing commonalities with Procter & Gamble.

Absolute cost barriers are the third, and from Bain's study the least important, type of barrier. The principal sources of these advantages appear to be (1) control of superior production techniques either by patents or by secrecy; (2) exclusive ownership by established firms of superior deposits of resources required in production; (3) the inability of entrant firms to acquire necessary factors of production on terms as favorable as enjoyed by established firms; and (4) less favorable access of entrant firms to liquid funds for investment, reflected in higher effective interest costs or in simple unavailability of funds in the required amounts.[15] There are probably few ways in which conglomerate mergers may have an appreciable, systematic effect on absolute cost barriers— hence one cannot generalize about probable tendencies.

Types of Potential Entrants and Significance of Barriers.— We have now stated the conditions in which, by raising barriers that are already moderate to high, a conglomerate merger may tend to lessen competition. Given the existence of barriers in a market, are they equally meaningful to all potential entrants? That is, does a particular advantage enjoyed by an established firm impose the same magnitude of disadvantage to all potential entrants? Probably not. "Potential entrants" include (1) entirely new firms just starting economic life; (2) established firms in other markets which are considering the possibility of entering the market by diversifying internally; and (3) established firms in other markets which are considering entering the market by diversifying through merger.

The model in Chapter IV of the growth of the firm and inducements for internal and external diversification pointed out many implications for merger as frequently the avenue of easiest entry. Hines explains that entry is easier for established outside firms than for entirely new firms since under

---

[15] Bain, *op. cit.*, pp. 240–241.

any given cyclical conditions the ease of entry depends on four factors: (1) information about opportunities for profitable entry; (2) access to productive resources; (3) access to markets; and (4) ability to overcome immobilities and other frictions that slow the rate of adjustment. The ease of entry for the established firm through diversification would seem to be at least as great as the ease for the entirely new firm in *each* of the four factors,[16] and, as we noted in Chapter IV, frequently easier if effected through merger rather than internal investment.

Therefore, one must be careful in deducing implications for competition from a given "height" of barriers. Any given barrier to entry is least prohibitive of entry by merger, somewhat more effective as a deterrent to internal diversification, and most effective as a deterrent to entirely new firms. We offer no judgment whether it is good or bad that entry into some markets can be effected only by merger or internal expansion by established firms rather than by new firms. We note only that, by definition, the complete absence of barriers to entry in any market would mean that entry *is* possible for the entirely new firm. Also, we offer no judgments whether under any circumstances "completely free entry" is good or bad. Any economic, as opposed to a sociopolitical, answer to the latter question would need to be based on the economics of the particular market and industry.

CONGLOMERATE MARKET POWER
AND INCREASED COMPETITION

Decrease in the level of concentration

Any conglomerate merger that may substantially lower the level of concentration and barriers to entry, particularly when the levels are moderate to high, may increase competition.

---

[16] Howard H. Hines, "Effectiveness of 'Entry' by Already Established Firms," *Quarterly Journal of Economics*, LXXI (February, 1957), pp. 134-137.

Much of the difference between how a conglomerate merger may tend to increase competition and how it may tend to decrease competition lies in the relative position of the acquired firm. The considerations are the same in both cases. The meaning for competition of the probable increase in market share is the all-important difference. For example, in a moderately-to-highly concentrated market, a conglomerate merger with high conglomerate market power probably enables the acquired firm to increase its share of the market. If the acquired firm is at the time of the merger relatively small in a moderately-to-highly concentrated market and if it acquires customers from all other firms in proportion to their size, then market concentration decreases. There is no reason to suppose the increased market share would not be drawn at least in part from the firms with the largest shares or indeed in approximate proportion to market share. Thus, if the latter took place the largest firms would suffer the greatest loss of market both absolutely and relatively. To the extent this occurred in a moderately-to-highly concentrated market, competition could be said to have been increased. Even if only a turnover among the largest firms resulted, we can say that competitive forces were operating.

We may summarize in a fifth proposition the general conditions in which a conglomerate merger may tend to increase competition by decreasing the level of concentration:

Proposition V

Given that the acquired firm has a relatively high magnitude of conglomerate market power and that it is relatively small in an already moderately-to-highly concentrated market, it is probable that the merger will decrease concentration, and, therefore, will tend to increase competition.

This proposition also applies to both homogeneous and differentiated goods and services. As discussed earlier, the conglomerate market power would be manifested in homogeneous markets differently from markets where the offerings and establishments can be differentiated.

Decrease in barriers to entry

Any conglomerate merger that may substantially lower the
level of barriers to entry, particularly when the levels are
moderate to high, may tend also to increase competition. How,
if at all, might a conglomerate merger decrease the level of
barriers to entry?

Let us look first at product-differentiation barriers. Recall
that a product-differentiation barrier is an advantage of extant firms over potential entrants because of the preference
of buyers for established firms' products. We saw in the analysis of increases in barriers to entry that (1) a high magnitude
of conglomerate market power tends to benefit the products
of the acquired firm; (2) if the high conglomerate market
power stems primarily from market profits, the products benefit primarily from high staying ability in promotion; (3) if
the high conglomerate market power stems as much or more
from marketing commonalities, the products of the acquired
firm will be enhanced by the staying ability and by the joint
marketing possibilities and resulting efficiencies. Thus, we
would expect as a result of persistent product or enterprise
promotion some switching of buyers to the acquired firm
(assuming its product was roughly comparable to the others
in price and quality). To the extent that the increased sales
come from customers previously brand-loyal to established
competitors there may be a less persistent loyalty for the
brands of those firms. However, this may or may not result in
a decrease in product-differentiation barriers. On the one
hand, if the merger makes current brand-loyal customers res-
tive and induces them to search among alternative brands,
then product-differentiation barriers are probably decreased
in the short run. On the other hand, if the merger makes current brand-loyal customers switch specifically and persistently
to the brands of the acquired firm, there is no reduction in the
total amount of buyer preference for specific brands in the
market. And in the latter case there is no reduction in product-
differentiation barriers.

Hence we are unable then to generalize about probable tendencies of conglomerate mergers to decrease product-differentiation barriers. It is just as difficult to generalize about conditions under which conglomerate mergers would probably systematically and appreciably decrease scale-economy barriers. We argued above that under certain conditions they probably would increase these barriers. But the reverse is difficult to conceive. Indeed, the barriers to entry inherent in real economies of scale appear to be ineradicable, short of legislating for enforced inefficiency.[17]

The same difficulty holds for conglomerate mergers and probable decreases in absolute-cost barriers. We can imagine instances of high-commonality mergers where the acquiring firm can introduce into the acquired firm substitute resource factors and production techniques enabling that firm and possibly other entrants to circumvent existing patents and other advantages of established firms. But such conjectures do not lend themselves to general assertions of probable tendencies.

SUMMARY AND CONCLUSIONS

Economists generally agree that the structure of the market in large part conditions the behavior of the firms in the market. A change in one or both of the two most important structure variables—level of concentration and level of barriers to entry—may suggest a change in the level of competition. In analyzing the probable competitive effects of conglomerate mergers—whether through conglomerate market power, reciprocity, or the elimination of potential competition—one generally must infer from the two structure variables. If the level of concentration and the level of barriers to entry are already moderate to high, then a conglomerate merger that tends to affect one or both of the variables may affect competition. That is, if the conglomerate merger tends to decrease the already moderate-to-high level, it may thereby

---

[17] See Bain, *op. cit.*, pp. 250–253.

also tend to increase competition in the market. On the other hand, if the level of one or both is moderate to high and if the conglomerate merger tends to increase the level, the merger may thereby tend to decrease competition in the market.

In the wealth-theory situations, it is frequently only a relatively high magnitude of conglomerate market power that can affect market structure. Many markets are characterized by differentiated oligopolies with at least some conglomerate market power. Furthermore, concentration and barriers both independently and in combination influence behavior. Thus, when both levels are high in a market characterized by differentiated oligopoly with at least some firms having conglomerate market power, a sizable "shock" must be injected into the market to alter its organization. Hence only a magnitude of conglomerate market power higher than most competitors' permits reasonably clear inferences at the time of the merger. The principle of how a conglomerate merger may affect competition remains the same, whether one is considering the effect on the variables separately or in combination.

The direction of change in one or both of the structure variables is a function of the relative position of the product in its market. Given a relatively high magnitude of conglomerate market power and already high levels of concentration and barriers, the relative position of the acquired firm (the special case for this analysis) is *the* critical factor in determining the probable competitive effects. Given the conditions stated in the preceding statement, an acquired firm that is relatively small in its market will probably decrease the level of concentration and therefore will tend to increase competition in that market. On the other hand, an acquired firm that is relatively large in its market will probably increase further the level of concentration and therefore tend to lessen competition.

The concept of conglomerate market power and the associated shifting of resources suggests implications for *any* postmerger market. To make the arguments clearer, we posed as the relevant market one of the acquired firm's markets. In the real world, however, resources *can be* and *are* shifted to any part of the conglomerate where the long-run profit opportunities are greatest.

In analyzing the probable competitive effects of conglomerate mergers, it is virtually never sufficient merely to note that a particular magnitude of conglomerate market power exists, or that reciprocity has occurred or is possible, or that a loss of potential competition has occurred. In the abstract, none of these has meaning for determining the effect of the conglomerate merger on competition.

All in all, then, the fundamental conclusion of this analysis is that conglomerate mergers are not inherently procompetitive or anticompetitive. Under some conditions they very probably can promote competition and under other conditions very probably decrease competition. The effect of conglomerate mergers on competition can be determined only by considering the probable changes in the characteristics of the pertinent market.

Appendix

STATUTORY
STANDARDS OF SECTION 7
AS AMENDED[1]

Stock

Stock acquisitions (a) by a corporation (b) of all, or part, of the stock or other share capital (c) of a corporation engaged in commerce, are covered.

Assets

Asset acquisitions (a) by a corporation subject to the jurisdiction of the F.T.C. (b) of all, or part, of the assets (c) of a corporation engaged in commerce, are also covered.

Direct and Indirect Acquisitions

Indirect, as well as direct, acquisitions of stock and assets are covered. The House Committee Report stated the Act, "forbids not only direct acquisitions but also indirect acquisitions, whether through a subsidiary or an affiliate or otherwise."

All, or Part, of the Stock or Assets

An acquisition of a part of a corporation's stock or assets is sufficient to bring the law into action, if the fraction is of a magnitude to effect the prohibited consequences.

Method of Acquisition

The Act covers not only the purchase of assets or stock, but also any other method of acquisition, *e.g.*, lease of assets.

---

[1] These statements of statutory standards are taken from Federal Trade Commission, *Report on Corporate Mergers and Acquisitions* (Washington: U.S. Government Printing Office, 1955), pp. 150–170, except as noted.

"Commerce"

Section 7 of the Clayton Act applies to all acquiring corporations, except those under the jurisdiction of specified regulatory agencies, regardless of whether the corporation is engaged in commerce. It does not apply unless the acquired corporation or the corporation whose stock or assets are acquired is engaged in commerce.

KINDS OF ACQUISITIONS NOT COVERED

Section 7 is not applicable to the following types of acquisitions even if they result in competitive consequences otherwise prohibited:

1. Acquisitions by noncorporations nor acquisitions by any person or organization not subject to the jurisdiction of the F.T.C.

2. Acquisitions from noncorporations.

3. Acquisitions solely for investment: Section 7 does not apply to corporations purchasing stock solely for investment and not using the stock, by voting or otherwise, to bring about, or attempt to bring about, a substantial lessening of competition.

4. Acquisitions under the authority of regulatory agencies.

5. Formation of subsidiaries: subsidiaries and branches are permitted so long as the effect of such formation is not substantially to lessen competition.

6. Acquisitions consummated prior to passage of the Act.

COMPETITIVE CONSEQUENCES COVERED

The 1950 Amendment is pointed toward acquisitions where in any line of commerce in any section of the country, the effect may be:

1. Substantially to lessen competition; or

2. To tend to create a monopoly.

[The words "may be" are significant. As Senate Report 1775, p. 6, stated, "A requirement of certainty and actuality of injury to competition is incompatible with any effort to supplement the Sherman Act by reaching incipient restraints."]

AMENDED SECTION 7 VIS-À-VIS ORIGINAL SECTION 7

The amended Section 7 differs from the earlier version of the Act in the following ways:

1. Acquisitions of assets as well as stocks, are covered.

2. Lessening of competition between the acquiring and acquired corporation is not necessary to a finding of violation. The elimination of the test of effect on competition between the acquiring and the acquired firm was to make it clear that the 1950 legislation was not intended to prohibit all acquisitions among competitors and also to make it clear that the bill applies to all types of mergers and acquisitions, vertical and conglomerate as well as horizontal which have the specified effects.

3. The law applies "In any Section of the Country rather than "In any Section or Community": the 1950 Act applies uniformly "in any line of commerce in any section of the country" where there may be a substantial lessening of competition or tendency to monopoly.

AMENDED SECTION 7 VIS-À-VIS SHERMAN ACT

Generally, the intent of the 1950 Act, as in other parts of the Clayton Act, is to cope with monopolistic tendencies in their incipiency—well before they have reached a stage that would justify a Sherman Act proceeding. Thus the 1950 Act is not intended as a "mere re-enactment" of the prohibitions of the Sherman Act, but is to extend to acquisitions not forbidden by the Sherman Act. It was underscored in the Committee hearings on H.R. 2734 that acquisitions of stock or assets may have a cumulative effect, and control of the market sufficient to constitute a violation of the Sherman Act may be achieved as the result of a series of acquisitions. Therefore the bill was intended to intercede in this cumulative process when the effect of an acquisition may be a reduction in the vigor of competition—although not so far-reaching as to amount to a combination in restraint of trade, creation of a monopoly, or an attempt to monopolize (which are of course the Sherman Act proscriptions).

Thus specifically:

1. The 1950 Act looks to probable future effects, not to actual and immediate effects; it applies to an incipient lessening of competition before any violation of the Sherman Act has occurred.

2. The question of whether an acquisition has, in fact, resulted in a substantial lessening of competition or a tendency to monopoly is not, therefore, at issue; no finding of actual restraint of trade

or of power to monopolize is necessary to a finding of violation of the 1950 Act.[2]

3. Nor is the intent of the acquiring or acquired company at issue: the House Committee explicitly stated that the Act differs from the Sherman Act in that it is unnecessary for the government to speculate as to the motive of those who promote a merger. Indeed, specific intent to impair competition, if combined with the power to injure competition, may, however, be taken into account in arriving at a judgement as to the probable effects of an acquisition.

4. Nor is it necessary to show predatory practices on the part of the acquiring company: the potential effect of an acquisition and not the past behavior of the acquiring company is what is tested.

5. Nor is it necessary that a specific acquisition be substantial: it suffices to note that an acquisition not substantial in itself, may impair competition substantially, if it is part of a cumulative process.

RELEVANT MARKETS

In that the 1950 Act applies to acquisitions where, "in any line of commerce, in any section of the country," the prohibited consequences may occur, it appears not to be limited to any specific set of product relations between the acquiring and acquired companies, to particular sets of suppliers, competitors, or customers of either company, or to any particular geographic area in which they may trade. Nor is scrutiny of the competitive effects of an acquisition confined to product lines which constitute a major portion of the business of either the acquiring or the acquired company. In effect, this would mean that market facts define the meaning of the relevant line of commerce and section of the country and that the actual and potential competitive consequences of an acquisition are to be tested (a) in any product line (line of commerce), (b) in any geographic area (section of the country), and (c) at whatever market levels (trade levels) they may occur.

---

[2] It is of course in regard to this point that a study of conglomerate-merger effects is so important. While it is clearly stated that it is unnecesary to find actual restraint of trade and so on, the administrative handling to date of conglomerate-merger cases frequently shows a reluctance to do otherwise—an understandable, however unfortunate, position.

ACQUISITIONS WITH INSUBSTANTIAL EFFECTS

Acquisitions which will not have substantial competitive consequences are not prohibited, specifically:

1. A corporation in failing or bankrupt condition is not prevented from selling its assets to a competitor.

2. Small companies are not prohibited from merging. In general, small companies are incapable of producing the specified effects on competition.

CONCERN WITH ECONOMIC ISSUES AND MARKET CONSEQUENCES[3]

The amended Section 7, being concerned with preventing incipient substantial lessening of competition through acquisitions from attaining realization, is necessarily interested in economic issues and market consequences. The proof of these consequences is in the domain of legal evidence, yet the facts to be considered are economic and statistical, and analysis of them is economic and statistical analysis. For the economist the problem is one of obtaining and analyzing economic data in forms that meet legal standards of relevance, materiality, and probative value.[4]

---

[3] The content of this section derives largely from the spirit of that of F.T.C. 1955, *op. cit.*, p. 148.

[4] See also U.S., Congress, House, Committee on the Judiciary, *Amending an Act Approved October 15, 1914*, 81st Cong., 1st Sess., 1949, H. Rept. 1191 to accompany H.R. 2734; U.S., Congress, Senate, Committee on the Judiciary, *Amending an Act Approved October 15, 1914*, 81st Cong., 2d Sess., 1950, Sen. Rpt. 1775; and *Report of the Attorney General's National Committee to Study the Antitrust Laws* (Washington, D.C.: U.S. Government Printing Office, 1955).

Bibliography

ARTICLES AND PERIODICALS

Adelman, M. A. "The Anti-Merger Act, 1950–1960," *American Economic Review*, LI (May, 1961).

——. "Business Size and Public Policy," *Journal of Business*, XXIV (October, 1951).

Andersen, Theodore A., *et al.* "Planning for Diversification Through Merger," *California Management Review*, I (Summer, 1959).

Andrews, Kenneth R. "Product Diversification and the Public Interest," *Harvard Business Review*, XXIX (July, 1951).

Bain, J. S. "Advantages of the Large Firm: Production, Distribution, and Sales Promotion," *Journal of Marketing*, XX (April, 1956).

Baldwin, William L. "The Motives of Managers, Environmental Restraints, and the Theory of Managerial Enterprise," *The Quarterly Journal of Economics*, LXXVIII (May, 1964).

Baumol, William. "The Theory of the Expansion of the Firm," *American Economic Review*, LII (December, 1962).

Bicks, Robert A. "Conglomerates and Diversification under Section 7 of the Clayton Act," *Antitrust Bulletin*, II (November-December, 1956).

Blair, John M. "The Conglomerate Merger in Economics and Law," *The Georgetown Law Journal*, XLVI (Summer, 1958).

Bok, Derek C. "Section 7 of the Clayton Act and the Merging of Law and Economics," *Harvard Law Review*, LXXV (December, 1960).

Brooks, Robert C., Jr. "Does Law Market Occupancy Indicate the Absence of Monopoly Power?", *Antitrust Bulletin*, IV (July-August, 1959).

——. "Price Cutting and Monopoly Power," *Journal of Marketing*, XXV (July, 1961).

———. "Volume Discounts as Barriers to Entry and Access," *The Journal of Political Economy*, LXIX (February, 1961).

Clark, Richard C. "Conglomerate Mergers and Section 7 of the Clayton Act," *Notre Dame Lawyer*, XXXVI (May, 1961).

Coase, R. H. "Monopoly Pricing with Interrelated Costs and Demands," *Economica*, New Series, XIII (November, 1956).

———. "The Nature of the Firm," *Economica*, New Series, IV (1937).

"Conglomerate Mergers under Section 7 of the Clayton Act," *The Yale Law Journal*, LXXII (May, 1963).

Conrad, Gordon R. "Unexplored Assets for Diversification," *Harvard Business Review*, XLI (September-October, 1963).

"The Consolidated Foods Case: A New Section 7 Test for the Conglomerate Merger," *Virginia Law Review*, XLIX (May, 1963).

Cyert, R. M. and March, J. G. "Organizational Structure and Pricing Behavior in an Oligopolistic Market," *American Economic Review*, XLV (March, 1955).

Day, Richard E. "Conglomerate Mergers and 'The Curse of Bigness,'" *North Carolina Law Review*, XLII (April, 1964).

Donnem, Roland W. "The Conglomerate Merger and Reciprocity," *Antitrust Bulletin*, VIII (March-April, 1963).

Edwards, H. D. "Price Formation in Manufacturing Industry and Excess Capacity," *Oxford Economic Papers*, New Series, VII (February, 1955).

Givens, Richard A. "Affirmative Benefits of Industrial Mergers and Section 7 of the Clayton Act," *Indiana Law Journal*, XXXVI (Fall, 1960).

Handler, Milton. "Emerging Antitrust Issues: Reciprocity, Diversification, Joint Ventures," *Virginia Law Review*, XLIX (April, 1963).

Heflebower, Richard B. "Corporate Mergers: Policy and Economic Analysis," *Quarterly Journal of Economics*, LXXVII (November, 1963).

———. "Economics of Size," *Journal of Business*, XXIV (October, 1951).

Hicks, J. R. "The Process of Imperfect Competition," *Oxford Economic Papers*, New Series, VI (February, 1954).

Hines, Howard H. "Effectiveness of 'Entry' by Already Established Firms," *Quarterly Journal of Economics*, LXXI (February, 1957).

Hirsch, W. A. "Toward a Definition of Integration," *The Southern Economic Journal*, XVII (October, 1950).

Holton, Richard H. "Price Discrimination at Retail: The Supermarket Case," *Journal of Industrial Economics*, VI (October, 1957).

Kaldor, Nicholas. "Market Imperfection and Excess Capacity," *Economica*, New Series, II (1935).

Lanzillotti, Robert F. "Multiple Products and Oligopoly Strategy: A Development of Chamberlin's Theory of Products," *Quarterly Journal of Economics*, LXVIII (August, 1954).

———. "Pricing Objectives in Large Companies," *American Economic Review*, XLVIII (December, 1958).

Loevinger, Lee. "Antitrust is Pro-Business," *Fortune*, LXVI (August, 1962).

———. "The Corporation as a Power Nexus," *Antitrust Bulletin*, VI (July-December, 1961).

Markham, Jesse W. "Antitrust Trends and New Constraints," *Harvard Business Review*, XLI (May-June, 1963).

———. "Merger Policy Under the New Section 7: A Six-Year Appraisal," *Virginia Law Review*, XLIII (May, 1957).

Mickwitz, Costa. "The Means of Competition at Various Stages of Production Distribution," *Kyklos*, II (1958).

Mueller, Willard F. "The Current Merger Movement and Public Policy," *Antitrust Bulletin*, VIII (July-August, 1963).

Nelson, Ralph L. "Market Growth, Company Diversification, and Product Concentration, 1947–1954," *Journal of the American Statistical Association*, LV (December, 1960).

Nutter, G. Warren. "Growth by Merger," *Journal of the American Statistical Association*, XLIX (September, 1954).

Osborn, Richard C. "Efficiency and Profitability in Relation to Size," *Harvard Business Review*, XXIX (March, 1951).

Papandreou, Andreas G. "Economics and the Social Sciences," *The Economic Journal*, LX (December, 1950).

Phillips, Almarin. "Concentration, Scale, and Technological Change in Selected Manufacturing Industries 1899–1939," *Journal of Industrial Economics*, IV (June, 1956).

Phillips, Charles F., Jr., and Hall, George R. "Economic and Legal

Aspects of Merger Litigation, 1951–1962," *University of Houston Business Review*, X (Fall, 1963).

———. "Merger Litigation, 1951–1960," *Antitrust Bulletin*, VI (January-February, 1961).

Robinson, Joan. "The Industry and the Market," *The Economic Journal*, LXVI (June, 1956).

Schwartzman, David. "Multiple-Company Mergers and the Theory of the Firm," *Oxford Economic Papers*, New Series, VII (June, 1955).

"Scott Paper Gets F.T.C. Ruling to Retain Three Acquired Firms Ordered Divested," *The Wall Street Journal* (April 24, 1964).

"Section 7 of the Clayton Act: A Legislative History," *Columbia Law Review*, LII (June, 1952).

"Statement of Walter Adams before the Joint Economic Committee of Congress, August 21, 1962," *Antitrust Bulletin*, VIII (March-April, 1963).

Staudt, Thomas A. "Program for Product Diversification," *Harvard Business Review*, XXXII (November-December 1954).

Stigler, George J. "The Case Against Big Business," *Fortune*, XLV May, 1952).

Stocking, George W., and Willard F. Mueller, "Business Reciprocity and the Size of Firms," *The Journal of Business*, XXX (April, 1957).

Wilcox, Clair. "From Economic Theory to Public Policy," *American Economic Review*, L (May, 1960).

Williamson, Oliver E. "Selling Expense as a Barrier to Entry," *Quarterly Journal of Economics*, LXXVII (February, 1963).

BOOKS

Bain, Joe S. *Barriers to New Competition*. Cambridge: Harvard University Press, 1956.

———. *Industrial Organization*. New York: Wiley, 1959.

———. *Pricing, Distribution and Employment*, rev. ed. New York: Henry Holt, 1953.

Baldwin, William L. *Antitrust and the Changing Corporation*. Durham: Duke University Press, 1961.

Berle, A. A., and Means, G. C. *The Modern Corporation and Private Property*. New York: Macmillan, 1932.

Bock, Betty. *Mergers and Markets: A Guide to Economic Analysis of Case Law,* 3rd ed. New York: National Industrial Conference Board, 1962.

Burns, A. R. *The Decline of Competition.* New York: McGraw-Hill, 1936.

Butters, J. K., J. Lintner, and W. Cary, *The Effect of Taxation on Corporate Merger.* Cambridge: Harvard University Press, 1951.

Chamberlin, E. H. (ed.). *Monopoly and Competition and Their Regulation.* London: Macmillan, 1954.

———. *The Theory of Monopolistic Competition,* 8th ed. Cambridge: Harvard University Press, 1962.

Clark, John M. *Competition as a Dynamic Process.* Washington, D. C.: The Brookings Institution, 1961.

———. *Studies in the Economics of Overhead Costs.* Chicago: University of Chicago Press, 1923.

Cook, P. Lesley. *Effects of Mergers.* London: Allen & Unwin, 1958.

Cyert, Richard M., and March, James G. *A Behavioral Theory of the Firm.* Englewood Cliffs, N. J.: Prentice-Hall, 1963.

Dean, Joel. *Managerial Economics.* Englewood Cliffs, N. J.: Prentice-Hall, 1951.

Dewey, Donald. *Monopoly in Economics and Law.* Chicago: Rand McNally, 1959.

Edwards, C. D. *Big Business and the Policy of Competition.* Cleveland: Western Reserve University Press, 1956.

———. *Maintaining Competition: Requisites of a Governmental Policy.* New York: McGraw Hill, 1949.

Foulke, Roy. *Diversification in Business Activity.* New York: Dun and Bradstreet, 1956.

Gort, Michael. *Diversification and Integration in American Industry.* Princeton: Princeton University Press for the National Bureau of Economic Research, 1962.

Heflebower, Richard B., and George W. Stocking, (eds.). *Readings in Industrial Organization.* American Economic Association. Homewood, Illinois: Richard D. Irwin, 1958.

Kaysen, Carl, and Donald F. Turner, *Antitrust Policy: An Economic and Legal Analysis.* Cambridge: Harvard University Press, 1959.

Lindahl, Martin L., and William A. Carter, *Corporate Concentration and Public Policy.* Englewood Cliffs, N. J.: Prentice-Hall, 1959.

Mace, Myles L., and George C. Montgomery, Jr. *Management Problems of Corporate Acquisitions.* Cambridge: Harvard University Press, 1962.

Machlup, Fritz. *The Economics of Sellers' Competition.* Baltimore: Johns Hopkins Press, 1955.

Martin, David D. *Mergers and the Clayton Act.* Berkeley and Los Angeles: University of California Press, 1959.

Mason, Edward S. *Economic Concentration and the Monopoly Problem.* New York: Atheneum, 1964. (First published in 1957 Cambridge: Harvard University Press.)

Miller, John (ed.). *Competition, Cartels, and Their Regulation.* Amsterdam: North-Holland, 1962.

National Bureau of Economic Research. *Business Concentration and Price Policy.* Princeton: Princeton University Press, 1955.

National Bureau of Economic Research. *Cost Behavior and Price Policy.* New York: National Bureau of Economic Research, 1943.

National Industrial Conference Board. *Economic Concentration Measures: Uses and Abuses.* New York: National Industrial Conference Board, 1957.

Papandreou, Andreas G., and John T. Wheeler, *Competition and Its Regulation.* Englewood Cliffs, N. J.: Prentice-Hall, 1954.

Penrose, E. T. *The Theory of the Growth of the Firm.* New York: Wiley, 1959.

Robinson, E. A. G. *The Structure of Competitive Industry.* Chicago: University of Chicago Press, 1958. (First published in 1931.)

Weston, J. Fred. *The Role of Mergers in the Growth of Large Firms.* Berkeley and Los Angeles: University of California Press, 1953.

Wilson, Charles H. *History of Unilever.* London: Cassell, 1954.

UNITED STATES GOVERNMENT PUBLIC DOCUMENTS

(Washington, D. C.: Government Printing Office)

Report of the Attorney General's National Committee to Study the Antitrust Laws. 1955.

Bureau of the Census. *Enterprise Statistics: 1958 Part 1 General Report.* 1963.

Congress. *The Present Trend of Corporate Mergers and Acquisitions.* Document 17. 80th Cong., 1st Sess., 1947.

Congressional Record. Vols. XCV, XCVI.

Federal Trade Commission. *News Summary.*

——. *Report on Corporate Mergers and Acquisitions.* 1955.

——. *The Merger Movement, A Summary Report.* 1948.

House of Representatives, Committee on the Judiciary. *Amending An Act Approved October 15, 1914.* Report No. 1191. 81st Cong., 1st Sess., 1949.

——. *Amending Sections 7 and 11 of the Clayton Act.* Report No. 596, 80th Cong., 1st Sess., 1947.

——. *Amending Sections 7 and 11 of the Clayton Act.* Report No. 1820. 79th. Cong., 2d Sess., 1946.

——. Select Committee on Small Business. *Mergers and Superconcentration.* 87th Cong., November 8, 1962.

——. Subcommittee of the Committee on the Judiciary. *Hearings on H.R. 2357.* 79th Cong., 1st Sess., 1945.

——. *Hearings on H.R. 515.* 80th Cong., 1st Sess., 1947.

——. *Hearings on H.R. 2734.* 81st Cong., 1st Sess., 1949.

——. *Hearings on Study of Monopoly Power,* Serial No. 14, Parts 1, 2-A, and a-B, 81st Cong., 1st Sess., 1949.

Senate, Committee on the Judiciary. *Amending An Act Approved October 15, 1914.* Report No. 1775. 81st Cong., 2d Sess., 1950.

——. Subcommittee of the Committee on the Judiciary. *Hearings on H.R. 2734.* 81st Cong., 1st and 2d Sess., 1949–1950.

——. Subcommittee on Antitrust and Monopoly of the Committee on the Judiciary. *Administered Prices: A Compendium on Public Policy.* 88th Cong., 1st Sess., 1963.

——. *Antitrust and Monopoly Activities.* 87th Cong., 1st Sess., 1961.

——. *Corporate Mergers and Acquisitions.* Report No. 132. 85th Cong., 1st Sess., 1957.

Temporary National Economic Committee. *Measurement of the Social Performance of Business.* Monograph No. 7, prepared by T. J. Kreps, 1940.

——. *Relative Efficiency of Large, Medium-sized, and Small Business.* Monograph No. 13, prepared by Myron Watkins. 1941.

——. *The Structure of Industry.* Monograph No. 27. 1941.

LEGAL HEARINGS AND CASES

Brown Shoe Co. et al. v. *U.S.* (370 U.S. 294).

Commerce Clearing House, Inc. *Trade Cases.* 1956–1964.

——. *Trade Regulation Reporter.* 1956–1964.

U.S. v. *Philadelphia National Bank* (374 U.S. 321).

UNPUBLISHED MATERIAL

Dydo, John S. "Inter-Industry Mergers, 1946–1954." Unpublished doctoral dissertation, University of California (Berkeley), 1962.

Elgass, George A. "The Multiline Firm in Relation to Competition." Unpublished doctoral dissertation, University of Michigan, 1956.

Mueller, Willard F. "Concentration and Mergers in American Manufacturing." Statement before the Subcommittee on Antitrust and Monopoly of the Committee on the Judiciary, United States Senate, July 2, 1964 (mimeographed).

Index

Lightning Source UK Ltd.
Milton Keynes UK
UKHW010053130822
407233UK00002B/215